New Accents

General Editor: TERENCE HAWKES

SCIENCE FICTION
ITS CRITICISM AND TEACHING

IN THE SAME SERIES

PATRICK PARRINDER

SCIENCE FICTION
ITS CRITICISM AND TEACHING

METHUEN
LONDON AND NEW YORK

First published in 1980 by
Methuen & Co. Ltd
11 New Fetter Lane, London EC4P 4EE
Published in the USA by
Methuen & Co.
in association with Methuen, Inc.
733 Third Avenue, New York, NY 10017

Typeset by Inforum Ltd, Portsmouth
Printed in Great Britain by
Richard Clay (The Chaucer Press) Ltd
Bungay, Suffolk

British Library Cataloguing in Publication Data
Parrinder, Patrick
  Science fiction. (New accents).
  1. Science fiction, English - History and criticism
  I. Title   II. Series
  823'.0876   PR830.S35

  ISBN 0-416-71390-4
  ISBN 0-416-71400-5 Pbk

For Darko and Robert:
Fellow-Wellsians, and pioneers of
the scholarly art surveyed in this book

CONTENTS

GENERAL EDITOR'S PREFACE

I T is easy to see that we are living in a time of rapid and radical social change. It is much less easy to grasp the fact that such change will inevitably affect the nature of those academic disciplines that both reflect our society and help to shape it.

Yet this is nowhere more apparent than in the central field of what may, in general terms, be called literary studies. Here, among large numbers of students at all levels of education, the erosion of the assumptions and presuppositions that support the literary disciplines in their conventional form has proved fundamental. Modes and categories inherited from the past no longer seem to fit the reality experienced by a new generation.

New Accents is intended as a positive response to the initiative offered by such a situation. Each volume in the series will seek to encourage rather than resist the process of change, to stretch rather than reinforce the boundaries that currently define literature and its academic study.

Some important areas of interest immediately present themselves. In various parts of the world, new methods of analysis have been developed whose conclusions reveal the limitations of the Anglo-American outlook we inherit. New concepts of literary forms and modes have been proposed; new notions of the nature of literature itself, and of how it communicates are current; new views of literature's role in relation to society flourish. *New Accents* will aim to expound and comment upon the most notable of these.

In the broad field of the study of human communication, more and more emphasis has been placed upon the nature and function of the new electronic media. *New Accents* will try to identify and discuss the challenge these offer to our traditional modes of critical response.

The same interest in communication suggests that the series should also concern itself with those wider and anthropological and sociological areas of investigation which have begun to involve scrutiny of the nature of art itself and of its relation to our whole way of life. And this will ultimately require attention to be focused on some of those activities which in our society have hitherto been excluded from the prestigious realms of Culture. The disturbing realignment of values involved and the disconcerting nature of the pressures that work to bring it about both constitute areas that *New Accents* will seek to explore.

Finally, as its title suggests, one aspect of *New Accents* will be firmly located in contemporary approaches to language, and a continuing concern of the series will be to examine the extent to which relevant branches of linguistic studies can illuminate specific literary areas. The volumes with this particular interest will nevertheless presume no prior technical knowledge on the part of their readers, and will aim to rehearse the linguistics appropriate to the matter in hand, rather than to embark on general theoretical matters.

Each volume in the series will attempt an objective exposition of significant developments in the field up to the present as well as an account of its author's own views of the matter. Each will culminate in an informative bibliography as a guide to further study. And while each will be primarily concerned with matters relevant to its own specific interests, we can hope that a kind of conversation will be heard to develop between them: one whose accents may perhaps suggest the distinctive discourse of the future.

TERENCE HAWKES

ACKNOWLEDGEMENTS

T HIS book would not have been written had I not
had the opportunity of teaching science fiction,
an opportunity as yet litle afforded by British
universities. I am deeply grateful to my students at Concordia and McGill Universities in Montreal, and at the University of Illinois at Urbana-Champaign, for providing such enjoyable and instructive experiences.

Some parts of this book were read in MS by Marc Angenot, Eric Rabkin, and Mark Rose, as well as by the two friends to whom it is dedicated. I hope that I have sufficiently deserved their encouragement and learnt from their disapproval. I am grateful to Liz Cogell, Samuel R. Delany, George Guffey, and Mark R. Hillegas for various kindnesses and suggestions. In keeping with its theme of strangeness and familiarity, *Science Fiction* was written in three countries and, almost entirely, in other people's houses: I should like to thank Ian Fletcher, David Ketterer, and Michael and Elizabeth Shapiro for a hospitality which does not, of course, extend to responsibility for any subversive or mistaken ideas which they may have unwittingly allowed to be hatched under their roofs.

An earlier version of chapter 5 was given as a paper at the Eaton Conference on Science Fiction and Fantasy Literature, held at the University of California-Riverside in February 1979. An early draft for the analysis of *Solaris* in chapter 6 appeared in *Radical Science Journal* No. 5 (1977).

London   P.P.
October 1979

INTRODUCTION

If Gray's definition of Paradise, to lie on a couch, namely, and read new novels, come any thing near truth, no small praise is due to him, who, like the author of Frankenstein, has enlarged the sphere of that fascinating enjoyment.[1]

I T is not to be expected that either Gray or Walter Scott (the author of the 1818 review of *Frankenstein* quoted above) would have understood the sort of enjoyment that readers throughout the industrialized world find today in science fiction. Science fiction (or SF) could only have come to prominence in the twentieth century, with its sweeping social changes and its unveiling of the promises and threats of modern technology. The grounds of the appeal which this genre makes to its still-growing readership are those of entertainment and conceptual novelty. It is as if SF had taken the promise implicit in the term 'novel' – but so often belied by actual novels – and adopted it, in theory at least, as the first principle of its fictional worlds. Scott paid his tribute to the quality of novelty when he praised *Frankenstein* as an 'extraordinary tale', able to excite 'new reflections and untried sources of emotion'. This is what science fiction tries to do.

The rise of science-fiction studies

The term itself did not come into widespread use until the 1930s, so that the ostensible critical history of science fiction is a very recent one. For a long time reactions to the genre were conditioned by its existence as a brash, commercial mode of writing with its main outlet in pulp magazines. There was an absolute separation between the handful of 'mainstream' literary works which, if one cared to think about it, were science-fictional in essence (*The Time Machine, Brave New World, Nineteen Eighty-Four*, etc.), and the stories and novellas which appeared in the pulps.

In the early 1950s, avowed SF writers such as Ray Bradbury and John Wyndham began to attract a degree of public attention which was reflected in critical journals and even in classrooms. Science fiction came to be recognized as a distinct literary genre, largely because it had so insistently 'arrived' as a social phenomenon. Sociologists, psychologists, historians of ideas, and political scientists began to turn to it on the assumption that it was an important aspect of the 'signs of the times'. Had not its writers predicted the atomic bomb, the moon landings, and the growing influence of research and development over the fluctuations of world politics? Was not science fiction an inescapable projection of hopes and fears about the direction in which society was moving? Was its sheer popularity indicative of some great underground shift in cultural values – a new apocalypticism, perhaps, or a new occultism? Most of these investigators would have added, 'however worthless it may be by purely literary standards' – and, in fact, recognition of the artistic achievements of science fiction has probably been little advanced by the interest shown in it by the cultural pundits. Criticism is an essentially conservative discipline, which tends automatically to discount entertainment-value, novelty, and above all conformity to cultural fashions. In science fiction as elsewhere it is often right to do so; the mode of innovation and the level of enjoyment offered were frequently all too superficial. Nevertheless, the growth of organized science-fiction studies has occurred within the literary field, and its purpose is to establish the aesthetic significance of science fiction as well as its place among the changing forms of contemporary popular expression.

A great deal of popular culture flourishes on nostalgia.

The classical detective story arose as police forces and crime syndicates were becoming more professionalized and more anonymous. The western looks back on a frontier which has long since been tamed. Romantic love stories have lost none of their popularity as divorce has become more commonplace. Science fiction itself is, for trade purposes, bracketed together with heroic fantasy, a branch of the historical romance in which nostalgia for a lost age of individualism is accentuated by the evocation of a quasi-feudal world of sorcerers and kings. Yet SF is not a nostalgic form, being concerned with alternative possibilities and anticipations which, in some few cases, have actually been borne out. Although a significant proportion of the genre is concerned with matters other than space-travel, it is no accident that its growth to widespread popularity and influence has occurred in the decades in which men have begun to travel away from the Earth. It does not matter, in this context, whether we regard flights to the moon as an earnest of things to come or as the last triumphs of a self-consuming machine civilization; this question has been as much debated in science fiction as anywhere else. SF, as the forward-looking fiction of the 'space age', claims attention as a new kind of writing, taking up a growing share of the fiction market; and its claims are becoming increasingly hard to resist.

Comments on pulp-magazine science fiction from outside its immediate readership were for long preoccupied with its real or imagined badness. In 1953 at the City College of New York Sam Moskowitz taught what appears to have been the earliest science-fiction course.[2] At about the same time, a scattering of favourable references to the genre began to appear in academic literary criticism. C.S. Lewis made an informal analysis of its various sub-species in a talk given to the Cambridge University English Club in 1955. Northrop Frye made science fiction the subject of some brief but pregnant remarks in his *Anatomy of Criticism* (1957). Kingsley Amis's widely-read and controversial survey *New Maps of Hell* (1961) did much to make SF intellectually fashionable. The appearance of a body of science-fiction scholars was signified by the foundation in 1959 (two years before the first manned space-flight) of the journal *Extrapolation* as the organ of a special Modern Language Association seminar. From this time on, the number of books and articles steadily increased, the period of greatest expansion being the early and middle 1970s. As in most other developments in the genre since 1930, the United States took the lead, followed at a distance by Britain, Canada, the Soviet Union, Eastern Europe, France, Germany, and Italy.

The growth of science-fiction studies has coincided with a somewhat separate development: the emergence of a marked literary self-consciousness among SF writers. Of the nineteenth-century authors of 'scientific romances', Mary Shelley, Poe, Verne, and Wells left important statements as to their methods and objectives. The aims of magazines such as Hugo Gernsback's *Amazing Stories* and John W. Campbell's *Astounding Science Fiction* in the 1930s and 1940s were often set out in the form of editorial pronouncements. Nearly all SF writers at this time had been trained (where they had been trained at all) in science and engineering rather than the humanities. Critical commentary within the field did not get under way until the 1950s, when authors such as Damon Knight and 'William Atheling, Jr' (i.e. the novelist James Blish) emerged as regular and often outspoken reviewers for the magazines. Since that time, science-fiction novelists have become increasingly articulate about their craft, and the relationship between novelists and academics has become close and intricate. The more extrovert writers have, in general, responded with alacrity to invitations to academic conferences and symposia, which would be much duller affairs without them. SF writers have frequently responded – with puzzlement, gratitude, or frank dismay – to the growing pile of academic interpretations of their books. Many have accepted fellowships and have run creative writing workshops; a few, such as Jack

Williamson and James Gunn, have become full-time profes-
sors of literature. Despite perennial complaints that the
genre is becoming 'respectable', it would seem that the
benefits resulting from these developments far outweigh
any drawbacks. Most of the professional problems of the SF
writer today – financial insecurity, changing markets,
editorial conservatism, and the dangers of over-production
– have little connection with the incursions of teaching and
scholarship.

Science-fiction studies, then, is a new and thriving discipline which has already begun to influence the genre it
serves. Its defects – which I would not wish to underempha-
size – are those of literary criticism itself at a time when the
purpose and *raison d'être* of this activity have too often been
obscured by its subsidiary functions of promoting academic
careers and justifying the money spent on 'research'. The
result is that text-books, articles, dissertations, biblio-
graphies, and scholarly reprints of SF material now appear
with bewildering rapidity. Genuinely innovative criticism of
SF is much rarer, though some of this precious commodity
certainly exists. The fate of science-fiction studies in the
immediate future may be more crucial than that of certain
of the more venerable branches of literary scholarship, since
the future achievements of the genre itself must inevitably
be affected by the (true or false) expectations aroused by its
critics.

Genre criticism

A book attempting to define science fiction and to situate it
with respect to earlier literary forms belongs under the
heading of 'genre criticism'. In the present confused state of
literary theory, it is not surprising that there are several
competing accounts of what genre criticism is. One of these,
associated with the Parisian critic Tzvetan Todorov, holds

that it is a theoretical pursuit in which *a priori* classifications are elaborated on purely logical grounds. The aim is to produce a poetics of narrative in which a series of rigorous structural models could be shown to generate all existing (and future) texts. The theorist's primary task is that of elaborating the models, rather than of demonstrating their usefulness in tracing the actual history of texts.[3] While this may be a corrective to the unthinking pragmatism of some Anglo-American scholarship, it will not escape the science-fiction critic that the elaboration of models constitutes only a part of the process of scientific enquiry. Any dogmatic attempt to detach the task of the theorist from that of the literary historian is likely to lead to sterility.

Another current approach is that which views a literary genre as being constituted by a series of linguistic practices, so that genre criticism may be reduced to a branch of semiotics. It is true (as will be discussed in chapter 6) that certain modes of language-use are characteristic of science fiction. Yet semiotics will not solve the peculiar problem of genre studies, which arises from the actual historical existence of the methods of classification that it explores. Both the theoretical critic and the semiotician are likely to have some trouble in showing that science fiction, as they would define it, is the same animal as the genre which goes under that name for its writers and readers. To date, linguistic and semiotic analyses of literary works have mostly been confined to familiar, 'mainstream' texts, whether of the classical-realist or experimental-modernist type. A substantial consensus about the broad nature and standing of the text is one of the unwritten assumptions behind such analyses. It is my belief that the generic considerations discussed in this book should come *before* any full-scale attempt to compile a 'narratology' of science fiction.

Science Fiction: Its Criticism and Teaching is intended both to elucidate science fiction's generic identity and to review the various critical (and, in the final chapter, pedagogic) approaches which have been taken to it. Chapter 1 sketches the growth of the genre's present sense of identity, while chapter 2 discusses its sociology. The following chapters, which approach SF from the viewpoint of romance, fable, and epic, make no attempt to reduce it to these traditional genres, still less to any one of them. Instead, like other modern kinds of narrative, science fiction consistently innovates upon the older forms to which it may be referred. I have been more concerned with trying to describe such innovations, and with the critical observations that may be drawn from them, than with the conventional proprieties of literary categorization. It is for the interested reader to decide how similar to other modern versions of 'romance', 'fable', and 'epic' are the elements of those forms that I shall locate in science fiction. Certainly they have been put forward in the belief that the 'new reflections' prompted by this quintessentially modern species of narrative will prove to have wide implications for literary criticism and cultural history.

1 WORKING DAYDREAMS, WORKSHOP DEFINITIONS

THE idea of literature is unthinkable without the conception of genres, or conventional literary forms. Many of the forms which still dominate our literature go back to the beginnings of Western civilization; these include the lyric, the drama, the satire, and the fable. Others, such as the novel, the crime story, and science fiction, came to prominence in very recent times. To refer to these new classes of writing as genres is to make a double assertion. At the very moment of insisting on their novelty and modernity, we imply that they have precursors and a history, that the contemporary practice is a combination of elements (which can now be seen with a new understanding) in the literary past.

Science fiction, though in many ways a highly conventional kind of writing, is one that cannot be defined uncontroversially. At first glance, it might appear to invite self-evident definition, as detective fiction is fiction about detectives and the art of solving crimes. Yet this is not the case, as is proved by the innumerable attempts that have been made to define it. On close inspection science fiction turns out to be a highly self-conscious genre: that is, the way it has been defined has an unusually close and symbiotic relationship with the way it has been written. For this reason, the question 'What is science fiction?' will be initially answered by looking at the critical history of the term itself and of its antecedents. Definitions of science fiction are not so much a series of logical approximations to an elusive ideal, as a small, parasitic sub-genre in themselves.

'Science Fiction' owes its name – though certainly not, as has sometimes been claimed, its existence – to Hugo Gernsback. Gernsback invented the term 'scientifiction' in 1926 to characterize the contents of *Amazing Stories*, one of the many magazines that he edited. Three years later, he switched to the more euphonious 'science fiction'. The widespread adoption of the latter term is signalized by the re-christening of the rival magazine *Astounding Stories* (originally *Astounding Stories of Super-Science*) as *Astounding Science Fiction* in 1938. For many years after this the term remained exclusively attached to magazine fiction and to the anthologies which reprinted such fiction; it was only in the 1950s that the SF label began to be applied to paperback novels.

From the start Gernsback had insisted, both in editorials and through the medium of a shrewdly commercial reprint policy, that the precursors of 'science fiction' were Edgar Allan Poe, Jules Verne, and H.G. Wells. In other words, there was a direct and acknowledged continuity between twentieth-century SF and the nineteenth-century tradition of the 'scientific romance'. Even the term 'science fiction', we now know, was not of Gernsback's invention. Scholars have recently traced it back to a long-forgotten tract of 1851, William Wilson's *A Little Earnest Book upon a Great Old Subject*, which predicts the spread of a new form of didactic literature:

> [Thomas] Campbell says that 'Fiction in poetry is not the reverse of truth, but her soft and enchanting resemblance.' Now this applies especially to Science-Fiction, in which the revealed truths of Science may be given interwoven with a pleasing story which may itself be poetical and *true* – thus circulating a knowledge of the Poetry of Science clothed in a garb of the Poetry of Life.[1]

In Wilson's use of the term, as in Gernsback's, there is a blend of prediction and retrospection, of the new and the old. The idea that the truths of science could be interwoven in a pleasing story was soon to receive its most thorough-going realization in the early novels of Jules Verne – novels packed with useful knowledge in the fields of engineering, astronomy, physics, geology, zoology, oceanography, palaeontology, and other sciences. Wilson, however, seems blind to the speculative and prophetic potential of such romances, and his idea of science fiction sounds a lot duller and more orthodox than the reality of a Verneian 'extraordinary voyage'. In fact, to speak of the 'Poetry of Science' as something altogether separate from the 'Poetry of Life' was already old-fashioned in 1851, when the industrial revolution had reached the stage at which science was visibly changing life. Such a development had been anticipated fifty years earlier by William Wordsworth, in a passage from the Preface to *Lyrical Ballads* which is perhaps the most famous of all pronouncements on the 'Poetry of Science':

> If the labours of Men of science should ever create any material revolution, direct or indirect, in our condition, and in the impressions which we habitually receive, the Poet will sleep then no more than at present; ... The remotest discoveries of the Chemist, the Botanist, or Mineralogist, will be as proper objects of the Poet's art as any upon which it can be employed, if the time should ever come when these things shall be familiar to us, and the relations under which they are contemplated by the followers of these respective sciences shall be manifestly and palpably material to us as enjoying and suffering beings. If the time should ever come when what is now called science, thus familiarised to men, shall be ready to put on, as it were, a form of flesh and blood, the Poet will lend his divine spirit to aid the transfiguration, and will welcome the Being thus produced, as a dear and genuine inmate of the household of man.

Despite its visionary rhetoric, this is again a highly conservative statement, though its conservatism is of a different kind from Wilson's. Guided by a naturalistic aesthetic of poetry as a record of men's actual impressions and feelings, Wordsworth does not see it as the poet's duty to anticipate the coming scientific revolution, but to wait until it is ready to put on a 'form of flesh and blood'. Nor does he doubt that this form will be benign – a gentle house-guest rather than a Frankenstein's monster. His commitment to the human nature that he believed he saw around him was, in fact, so rock-like that he could only allow the subject-matter of science into poetry once it had become 'familiarized'. Yet even so classically-minded a critic as Samuel Johnson, in the *Preface to Shakespeare* (1765), had recognized the claims of that sort of literature which takes hold of the strange and *makes* it familiar:

> *Shakespeare* approximates the remote, and familiarizes the wonderful; the event which he represents will not happen, but if it were possible, its effects would probably be such as he has assigned.

Accounts of wonders and marvels have a venerable place in literature itself, if not always in critical discussion. The emergence of an aesthetic outlook bringing together the ideas of the 'Poetry of Science' and the familiarization of the wonderful was one of the fruits of the late-eighteenth-century taste for the Gothic – a taste which both Johnson and Wordsworth deplored. The Gothic preoccupation with the sensational and the exotic lies behind the immediate predecessor of science fiction, the nineteenth-century 'scientific romance'.

The scientific romance

Scientific romance at its simplest consists in the use of scientific (or, more often, quasi-scientific) elements in highly-coloured romantic fiction. Perhaps the best-known examples are Nathaniel Hawthorne's tales, such as 'The

Birthmark' (1843) and 'Rappaccini's Daughter' (1844), in which the gruesome labours of a demonic scientist serve to blight the happiness of the hero or heroine. Similarly, in Fitz-James O'Brien's 'The Diamond Lens' (1858), Linley, the 'mad microscopist', constructs a perfect microscope which enables him to see the interior of the atom. As he increases the magnification, the water-drop on his slide is resolved into the apparition of a beautiful female, Animula, who of course is doomed to shrivel and disappear as the water evaporates. Hawthorne, O'Brien, and their many followers are not so much science-fiction writers as romancers dabbling in the scientific exotic. It is when an author becomes conscious of an obligation to bring the 'Poetry of Science' within the sphere of the probable that we approach science fiction proper. As Scott wrote in his review of *Frankenstein*:

> In this view, the *probable* is far from being laid out of sight even amid the wildest freaks of imagination; on the contrary, we grant the extraordinary postulates which the author demands as the foundation of his narrative, only on condition of his deducing the consequences with logical precision.[2]

In many ways *Frankenstein*, like 'Rappaccini's Daughter' and 'The Diamond Lens', is written in the mode of 'scientific romance'. The monstrous creature pining for a mate, and the slaughter of Frankenstein's bride on her wedding-night, are prime examples of Gothic eroticism. Yet the original preface to *Frankenstein* (reportedly written by Mary's husband Percy Shelley) joins with Scott in emphasizing that this is no supernatural tale of uncontrolled horrors:

> The event on which this fiction is founded has been supposed, by Dr Darwin and some of the physiological writers of Germany, as not of impossible occurrence. I shall not be supposed as according the remotest degree of serious faith to such an imagination; yet, in assuming it as the basis of a work of fancy, I have not considered myself as merely weaving a series of supernatural terrors. The

event on which the interest of the story depends is exempt from the disadvantages of a mere tale of spectres or enchantment. It was recommended by the novelty of the situations which it develops, and however impossible as a physical fact, affords a point of view to the imagination for the delineating of human passions more comprehensive and commanding than any which the ordinary relations of existing events can yield.

Whatever we make of *Frankenstein* itself, the preface unmistakably claims for it the status of science fiction. The whole story is said to depend on a single 'event', the creation of human life in the laboratory, which certain scientists have alleged to be possible. (Mary Shelley had in mind the recent discoveries in the field of atmospheric electricity and galvanism, and Erasmus Darwin's observations of the activity of bacteria in dead vegetable matter.) But the possibility of reanimating a corpse is viewed hypothetically, in a mood of wary scepticism rather than credulity. *Frankenstein* is thus a piece of speculative fiction which does not rely on mythmaking or supernatural terrors to get its effects. The author has preserved 'the truth of the elementary principles of human nature', even though she does not scruple to 'innovate upon their combinations'. The result is a tale which looks at human life from a distanced and (to use the modern term) estranged point of view, one not available to realistic fiction with its 'ordinary relations of existing events'. While this interpretation of *Frankenstein* unquestionably plays down the more lurid and romantic aspects of the story, the preface may be allowed to stand in its own right as an aesthetic statement closely anticipating modern theories of the science-fiction genre. It is with this brief manifesto that the self-consciousness of science fiction might be said to begin.

After Mary Shelley, it is true, there is a prolonged gap. Although the scientific romance played a minor if under-appreciated part in the output of such writers as Hawthorne, Melville, and Mark Twain, and although the popularity of the form dramatically increased in the later Victorian decades, it did not undergo systematic development until the work of Jules Verne and H.G. Wells. Verne's most important predecessor was Edgar Allen Poe, whose note to 'The Unparalleled Adventure of One Hans Pfall' (1835) claims priority in the 'application of scientific principles (so far as the whimsical nature of the subject would permit) to the actual passage between the earth and the moon'.[3] Poe's attachment to *'verisimilitude'*, however, is as deceptive as that of earlier satirist like Swift in *Gulliver's Travels*. The more he protests it, the greater is the reader's suspicion of being the victim of an outrageous hoax. (Thus the critic David Ketterer argues that, far from successfully completing his balloon-voyage to the moon, Hans Pfall is actually blown to pieces at the moment of take-off.)[4] Nothing in Poe's world is plausible in the sense that the adjective may be applied to Verne, who set his face against 'irresponsible' scientific speculation and confined himself, for the most part, to short-range extrapolations from existing knowledge and existing technology. The type of naturalism pursued in his 'extraordinary voyages' is brought out in his much-quoted dismissal of Wells's *The First Men in the Moon*:

> I make use of physics. He invents. I go to the moon in a cannon-ball, discharged from a cannon. Here there is no invention. He goes to Mars in an airship, which he constructs of a material which does away with the law of gravitation. *Ça c'est très joli* . . . but show me this metal. Let him produce it.[5]

Not only has Verne apparently confused *The First Men in the Moon* with another contemporary space-voyage, but his mode of space-travel now seems no less impossible than Wells's. Nevertheless, Verne's fiction is a logical extension of the engineering mentality of the Age of Steam. It is probably quite superfluous to effect a rigid separation between his 'scientific' fiction and a non-science-fictional travel epic such as *Around the World in Eighty Days*. The romanticization

of science accomplished in his novels is somewhat superficial, given that his submarines, airships and space projec-
tiles can all be traced back to contemporary prototypes and
blueprints. Verne's fiction today is being rescued from the
status of boys' fiction to which it has long been confined, but
recent critics have emphasized the quality of his social and
mythical, rather than his strictly scientific, imagination.

Although both Verne and Wells have usually been
described as authors of scientific romances, their achievement – above all, that of Wells – was to free science fiction
from its initial dependence on the romance form. The
lineage of the nineteenth-century prose romance includes
the works of Scott, Hawthorne, Dumas, and Victor Hugo.
In the late Victorian period these writers were succeeded,
not only by bestselling entertainers like Rider Haggard and
Stanley J. Weyman, but by such self-conscious literary artists
as William Morris and Robert Louis Stevenson.

Stevenson is the most persuasive of the nineteenth-
century apologists for romance, which he sees as a necessary
reaction to the ascendancy of realistic and naturalistic (or, as
they were often described, 'scientific') attitudes in fiction.
His outburst, in a letter to Henry James, against the tyranny
of everyday detail suggests the extent to which he thought of
realism as a curb placed on the free-ranging imagination:
'How to get over, how to escape from the besotting *particularity* of fiction. "Roland approached the house; it had green
doors and window blinds; and there was a scraper on the
upper step." To hell with Roland and the scraper!'[6] Against
the Jamesian aesthetic of 'solidity of specification', Stevenson is the spokesman of 'significant simplicity', of a
stripping-down of fiction to the essential elements which
make up the adventure-story and the fairy-tale. The mark
of great writing, he argues in 'A Gossip on Romance' (1882),
is to

> satisfy the nameless longings of the reader, and to obey
> the ideal laws of the day-dream. The right kind of thing
> should fall out in the right kind of place; the right kind of
> thing should follow; and not only the characters talk aptly

and think naturally, but all the circumstances in a tale answer one to another like notes in music.

It is possible to share the impatience with Zolaesque realism that Stevenson expresses in such essays as 'A Note on Realism' (1883) without being more than momentarily beguiled by his ideal of the romance. His ideal reader appears to be a juvenile reader, totally absorbed in an illusory world of 'clean, open-air adventure' told in words which 'run . . . in our ears like the noise of breakers'.[7] This is a soothing and nostalgic, not a challenging ideal, and it seems to confuse the 'timelessness' of great art with the temporal suspension of the daydream.

Stevenson came nearest to science fiction in *Dr Jekyll and Mr Hyde* (1886), a proto-Freudian romance of the 'war in the members' of the human frame which is undoubtedly serious in subject, if not in treatment. *Dr Jekyll and Mr Hyde* is a near-classic case of a fantasy drawing on scientific themes which should nevertheless be excluded from the category of science fiction.[8] Dr Jekyll, the epitome of Victorian respectability, transforms himself into the shape of the criminal Hyde as the result of taking a chemical concoction. The transformation defies physiological explanation and, in addition, it is not caused by the otherwise harmless drug but by an unknown impurity. Eventually, Jekyll finds himself degenerating into Hyde willy-nilly and without chemical assistance. At this point we do not doubt that we are reading an allegory of a species of diabolic possession rather than a science-fiction story. Stevenson's use of a laboratory atmosphere is simply one of the many layers of mystification with which the central character is surrounded. The novel is a remarkable attempt to exploit the melodramatic conventions of the age in such a way as to expose Victorian hypocrisy and self-division. Its science-fictional trappings, however, are a rather transparent concession to the 'besotting particularities' of late-nineteenth-century life. They are neither coherent in themselves, nor do they in any way affect the nature of Stevenson's allegory.

Logical speculation: H.G. Wells

It may be noted that *Dr Jekyll and Mr Hyde* is no more acceptable as a detective story, in the tradition of Poe and Conan Doyle, than it is as science fiction. Both science fiction and the classical detective story can be seen to define themselves by their opposition to Stevensonian 'timeless' romanticism. For the 'ideal laws of the day-dream' they substitute a detailed account of its material conditions. The logical and rational attitude of science fiction takes up the reader's 'nameless longings' with the intention of showing just how and why they might become actual, and what their unforeseen – and often highly unpleasant – consequences might be. The result is not primarily an 'aesthetic' fiction, aiming to delight the reader's sensibility, but rather a working model of an alternative reality. One of the places where this is most evident is in the utopian writings of the late nineteenth century. There are different kinds of rationality, and different ways in which it may be embodied in fiction; if nothing else, the contrast between the technological anticipations of Edward Bellamy's *Looking Backward* (1888), and the combination of romance with visionary politics in William Morris's *News from Nowhere* (1890), would show this. Yet the crucial point is that in the utopian fictions of both Bellamy and Morris, romance enters the domain of political philosophy and becomes associated with ideological struggle. Similarly, H.G. Wells's 'romances' express a scientific philosophy, and their narrative framework is underpinned by a direct intellectual appeal to the reader, rather than by psychological allegory and symbolism. Their affinities are as much with the satire and the realistic novel as with the romance proper.

Wells, who began publishing in the mid-1890s, is the pivotal figure in the evolution of the scientific romance into modern science fiction. His example has done as much to shape SF as any other single literary influence. This is partly because of his mastery of a range of representative themes (time-travel, the alien invasion, biological mutation, the future city, anti-utopia) and partly because his stories embody a new generic combination, which proved attractive both to 'literary' and to scientifically-minded readers. By the time that he made his most influential contribution to the definition of science fiction, in his Preface to the 1933 edition of his *Scientific Romances*, his example had been studied and copied for over thirty years. The 1933 Preface, indeed, is anachronistic in that it betrays no awareness of the popular SF magazines, although Wells himself was aware of their existence, and had engaged in a prolonged and unsatisfactory correspondence with Hugo Gernsback over the appropriate fees for reprinting his work.[9] Wells had no objection to letting his popularity with the *Amazing Stories* readership help to pay his bills, but, in the context of a discussion which stresses the high antiquity of his brand of science fiction, he evidently felt the opportunist antics of the pulps to be beneath his dignity.

In his essay Wells distinguishes between the Verneian 'anticipation' of future possibilities, based on extrapolation from contemporary social and technological trends, and the purely hypothetical scientific 'fantasy'. Although he himself had significantly contributed to the first type of story (as his reputation as a prophet of the tank, the atom bomb and aerial warfare indicates), his major science fiction belongs to the second category. In his account of these works he contrasts the purely speculative nature of the hypotheses on which they are based with the rigour with which he pursues the consequences of these hypotheses. The initial premise requires of the reader no more than the willing suspension of his disbelief; as the narrator of *The Time Machine* says to his hearers, 'Take it as a lie – or a prophecy. Say I dreamed it in the workshop.' Though backed up by a display of scientific patter, the premise, whether of time-travel, invisibility or (to take more recent examples) teleportation or telepathy, is comparable to the traditional marvels of magic and fairy-tale. Once the premise is granted, however, its consequences are explored in a spirit of rigorous realism:

In all this type of story the living interest lies in their non-fantastic elements and not in the invention itself. . . .

The thing that makes such imaginations interesting is their translation into commonplace terms and a rigid exclusion of other marvels from the story. Then it becomes human. . . . As soon as the magic trick has been done the whole business of the fantasy writer is to keep everything else human and real. Touches of prosaic detail are imperative and a rigorous adherence to the hypothesis. Any *extra* fantasy outside the cardinal assumption immediately gives a touch of irresponsible silliness to the invention. So soon as the hypothesis is launched the whole interest becomes the interest of looking at human feelings and human ways, from the new angle that has been acquired.

The significance of Wells's contribution to the definition of SF lies in this combination of fantasy and realism. In scientific terms the restrained fantasy that he advocates is reminiscent of the controlled experiment, in which the variables at work are subjected to rigorous analysis and only one variable is changed at a time. His statement in the Preface that 'Nothing remains interesting where anything may happen' may be compared with the Occam's Razor principle that 'entities should not be multiplied beyond necessity'. Nevertheless, the excitement of Wells's best science fiction lies in the process by which the original premise is combined with further, more genuinely scientific premises to produce conclusions which seem increasingly fantastic, though the reader is convinced by the narrative rhetoric that they are logical and necessary. The idea of a 'single premise' fantasy consisting of no more than a displaced realism does not do justice to this process, in which new elements and considerations (none of which, however, appears as gratuitous as the original hypothesis) are progressively introduced to provide a deepening sense of speculation and mental experiment.

The fiction of the magazines

Wells's 1933 Preface ends on a note of disillusion, suggesting that in the light of the Great War and the rise of Hitler he had come to regard his earlier science fiction as largely escapist: 'The world in the presence of cataclysmal realities has no need of fresh cataclysmal fantasies.' In science fiction, too, this was the end of an era. Wells's is the last of the old-style, 'literary' definitions of this form of writing, the last which could afford to ignore both Gernsback's term and the cultural phenomenon that it was coming to represent. The American magazines, for one thing, did not share Wells's gloom about the immediate future. In them, commitment to scientific values was becoming synonymous with a near-euphoric fascination with the prospects of technology such as Wells had felt in the early years of this century In commercial terms, Gernsback and his successors showed that stories embodying social change, providing that they offered a Verne-like combination of boyish adventure with nuts, bolts and blueprints, could more than hold their own against other descendants of the nineteenth-century romance such as the mass-produced tales of horror and supernatural fantasy. Gernsback's editorial for the first number of *Science Wonder Stories* (June 1929) stated his intention of rejecting all stories outside the realm of scientific possibility: 'It is the policy of *Science Wonder Stories* to publish only such stories that have their basis in scientific laws as we know them, or in the logical deduction of new laws from what we know.' A panel of experts was being formed, he added, to pronounce on the scientific correctness of the stories submitted.[10]

Gernsback's enthusiasms are sufficiently indicated by the titles of some of his other magazines: *Modern Electrics, Air Wonder Stories, Science and Invention*. (One of his main interests was in promoting the sale of crystal sets.) He is without doubt a representative figure, even though the originality of his contribution to SF history has at times been grossly overrated. The rough-and-ready critical terminology which has grown up within the 'ghetto' of popular SF owes much to the emphasis on scientific correctness and technological forecasting in his magazines. Stories devoted to the technological outlook for man and his possible ways of meeting new physical challenges (above all, those of space-travel) came to be known as 'hard' or 'engineer's' science fiction. Where the social and human sciences, or those of other races, were involved, it became customary to speak of 'soft' or speculative SF. Other recognized kinds of story were 'science fantasy', in which the science was likely to be transparently pseudo rather than genuine, and the melodramatic and comparatively non-intellectual 'space opera'.

Despite some recent attempts, the project of basing a comprehensive rhetoric of science fiction on these highly ambiguous categories is hopeless. (The *reductio ad absurdum* of this sort of critical empiricism would presumably involve some benighted researcher in distinguishing between the literary categories of the 'amazing', the 'astounding' and the 'weird' on the basis of the publication policies of *Amazing Stories*, *Astounding Science Fiction* and *Weird Tales*.) If one looks at the sociology and economics of magazine fiction it is readily understandable that the writers' anxiety to get published, the editors' tedious task of wading through piles of semi-literate manuscripts, and the taxonomic instincts of the fans all led to reliance upon formulas and categories which disregard the many-sidedness of any really complex use of science fiction or fantasy. In the so-called 'golden age' of the magazines it seems to have been widely assumed that writing science-fiction stories was as simple and saleable a skill as the ability to tune a carburettor. The commercialism of magazine fiction is typified by Lloyd Arthur Eshbach's *Of Worlds Beyond: The Science of Science Fiction Writing* (1947), a manual for potential writers which sets out both the tricks of the trade and the dollar value of learning its mysteries. In this volume the editor of *Astounding Science Fiction*, John W. Campbell, Jr, writes that the act of buying a magazine is tantamount to 'hiring an author', while Jack Williamson repeats Wells's prescription for fantasy founded on a single basic premise, emphasizing that this is the best way to a 'publishers cheque'.

Of the critical terms which arose in the magazine era, the only two which appear to be definable with reasonable precision are 'hard' science fiction and 'space opera'. 'Hard' SF is related to 'hard facts' and also to the 'hard' or engineering sciences. It does not necessarily entail realistic speculation about a future world, though its bias is undoubtedly realistic. Rather, this is the sort of SF that most appeals to scientists themselves – and is often written by them. The typical 'hard' SF writer looks for new and unfamiliar scientific theories and discoveries which could provide the occasion for a story, and, at its more didactic extreme, the story is only a framework for introducing the scientific concept to the reader. In 'space opera' (the analogy is with the Western 'horse opera' rather than the 'soap opera') the reverse is true; a melodramatic adventure-fantasy involving stock themes and settings is evolved on the flimsiest scientific basis. SF films, TV serials and comic strips are normally of this type. It is commonly supposed (though Samuel R. Delany has recently questioned this assumption)[11] that space opera would not undergo any essential alteration if its ray-guns were turned into six-guns and Princess Lia's battle-squadron into the sheriff's posse. Certainly there is a level of response at which the similarities between commercial westerns, war films and a large proportion of popular SF are more striking than the differences.

Extrapolation: Robert A. Heinlein

In some of the best magazine fiction of the 1940s and 1950s, fascination with the technological future merges into a broader and more critical concern with the nature of social change. The prospect of space-travel which was held out for mankind by Wells and other twentieth-century scientific prophets took form and substance as writers began to imagine the colonial prospects, the temptations of power, the military and scientific codes of behaviour and the possibilities of a relapse into barbarism that this new imperial mission was likely to breed. Robert A. Heinlein was perhaps the most influential of the writers who explored such prospects while claiming to present an essentially realistic picture of social development. Heinlein, indeed, viewed SF as

'Realistic Future-Scene Fiction' and suggested the following definition: 'realistic speculation about possible future events, based solidly on adequate knowledge of the real world, past and present, and on a thorough understanding of the nature and significance of the scientific method.'[12] Heinlein's commitment in this essay ('Science Fiction: Its Nature, Faults and Virtues', 1959) was to the didactic function of science fiction, which was 'preparing our youngsters to be mature citizens of the galaxy'. There is a hint of over-protestation in his definition; after all, he was prepared to argue that time-travel stories were admissible on the grounds that the nature of time was not yet scientifically understood. Heinlein always insisted on the 'speculative' nature of SF – thus anticipating the 'New Wave' writers of the 1960s who tried to re-christen the genre as 'speculative fiction' – but his definitions of the form all tend to suggest that the writer's concern is with logical forecasts or extrapolations from present trends. Although he makes it clear that SF is concerned with the human problems brought about by technological change, his definition of 'Realistic Future-Scene Fiction' makes it sound indistinguishable from the products of the so-called science of 'futurology'. The actual development of space-flight and the resulting demand for SF writers as media pundits and commentators did much to confirm their Heinleinian self-image as futurological prophets.

'In the speculative science fiction story', Heinlein wrote in 1947, 'accepted science and established facts are extrapolated to produce a new situation, a new framework for human action.'[13] Clearly the field of speculation was limited if it could be no more than extrapolation from established facts; there was no room for Wells's 'impossible hypothesis'. A slight modification of this position is suggested in an essay by John W. Campbell, which appeared alongside Heinlein's piece:

> To be science fiction, not fantasy, an honest effort at prophetic extrapolation of the known must be made. . . . Sociology, psychology and para-psychology are, today,

not true sciences; therefore instead of forecasting future results of applications of sociological science of today, we must forecast the *development of a science* of sociology.[14]

The projection of new sciences, as it turned out, would hardly be confined to such an orthodox candidate as sociology. One of the writers Campbell printed in *Astounding* was L. Ron Hubbard, later to become notorious as the inventor of 'dianetics' and the founder of the Church of Scientology.

The 'New Wave'

During the 1960s Heinlein's own fiction began to change to some extent, while a new generation of writers emerged to interpret the term 'speculative fiction' with a latitude that he can hardly have envisaged. Heinlein was typical of the SF writers who had learned their craft in the pulp magazines, and had followed it in self-confident isolation from any wider artistic trends. The organs of the so-called 'New Wave' – the British magazine *New Worlds* edited by Michael Moorcock, and the series of *Dangerous Visions* anthologies produced by Harlan Ellison – introduced a tone of knowingness and literary sophistication, with an almost obligatory commitment to formal experiment. The much-publicized cultural innovations of the 1960s, from the wave of psychedelic drugs and alternative life-styles to the Tolkien cult and the fantastic, 'postmodernist' fictional mode of novelists such as John Barth, Richard Brautigan, and Thomas Pynchon, all contributed to the sense that experience as a whole was becoming 'science-fictional' – though, of course, it was becoming rather more difficult to say what exactly such a statement might mean. The evident connections between J.G. Ballard's insistence that 'outer space' fiction was really a projection of inner space and the popular psychoanalytic theories of the decade are a case in point. (To add to the confusion, one might note that an eminent 'mainstream' novelist, Doris Lessing, began to write scientific fantasies embodying the theories of the leading anti-psychiatrist R.D. Laing.) No doubt a new area of surrealism and fantasy was annexed for serious fiction in the 1960s and early 1970s, and certain science-fiction writers such as Kurt Vonnegut, Jr contributed heavily to this postmodernist mode of contemporary expression. Nevertheless, it is significant that their progress has been regarded within the SF field as one of defection.

Perhaps the most representative 'orthodox' reaction to the rise and subsequent fall of the New Wave is to be found in James Blish's critical essays, published as *More Issues at Hand* by 'William Atheling, Jr' (1970). Blish's concern is to judge science fiction by the professional standards both of literature and of science. He welcomes SF's 'gradual re-assimilation . . . into the mainstream of literature'; this is both a sign of growing maturity and a warning to writers and fans who would like to keep the genre exempt from the 'usual standards of criticism'.[15] At the same time, Blish mounted a vigorous — and perhaps rather narrowly con-ceived — sanitary campaign against the spread of 'science fantasy' and 'mytholatry' in SF. The writers whom he attacks on this score, in essays written between 1960 and 1970, include Brian Aldiss, J.G. Ballard, Charles Eric Maine, and Roger Zelazny. Aldiss and Maine, for example, are accused of producing 'science-fantasy', 'a kind of hybrid in which plausibility is specifically invoked for most of the story, but may be cast aside in patches at the author's whim and according to no visible system or principle'.[16] Though he concedes that rather little SF may be wholly scientific in spirit, it is only with the advent of the New Wave that writers have deliberately set out to travesty the scientific imagina-tion.

In retrospect, it is not difficult to identify the exagger-ations of Blish's polemic. The New Wave both reflected (and to some extent anticipated) popular disillusionment with scientific advance, and expressed the anxiety of a group of young writers to take science fiction out of the mode estab-lished by Gernsback, Heinlein, and Campbell. Since SF has retained its familial identity, the episode of the New Wave now appears as part of the normal succession of literary generations. At the same time, science fiction has made enormous strides in complexity and self-awareness since Blish began his sanitary efforts in 1960. Those of the younger novelists who have done most to shape an awareness of their craft have done so by writing criticism which deliberately circumvents the old style of logical, simplistic definitions of SF. In *Billion Year Spree*, his vividly impressionistic history of the genre, Brian Aldiss refers to it as a 'search for a definition of man and his status in the universe which will stand in our advanced but confused state of knowledge (science) and is characteristically cast in the Gothic or post-Gothic mould'. This is not the language of someone whose main interest lies in generic demarcation, and, indeed, the onus of defending the coherence of science fiction as a literary category seems recently to have passed from writers and editors to academic theorists. Their impulse, as Samuel R. Delany notes, is to define the genre not as a group of themes and conventions but as 'a particular type of discourse, a particular sort of "word machine", that performs certain functions'[17] – that is, to define it not in terms of content but of literary structure. Such an attempt is justified by the heterogeneity of science fiction once it breaks away from the Verneian and Heinleinian modes of 'engineer's fiction', of linear extrapolation and the future history. Nor is it necessarily incompatible with the approach that is found in Wells's Preface to his scientific romances and, implicitly, in Shelley's Preface to *Frankenstein*.

Definition by structure

The problem of a structural approach is that SF has normally been defined in terms of its content: science. It is not difficult to show that the inclusion of science entails certain formal requirements, but the question is whether these are of major literary significance. For a story to be acceptable by the science-fiction magazines, the writer was expected to provide a scientific or quasi-scientific explanation of the technology innovations that he portrayed. Thus, to take a well-known example given by Frederic Brown in his introduction to *Angels and Spaceships* (1955), the Midas legend can be turned into SF provided that the faculty of turning everything you touch into gold can be explained as a new development in molecular physics:

> Mr Midas, who runs a Greek restaurant in the Bronx, happens to save the life of an extraterrestrial from a far planet who is living in New York anonymously as an observer for the Galactic Federation, to which Earth for obvious reasons is not yet admitted. . . . The extraterrestrial, who is master of sciences far beyond ours, makes a machine which alters the molecular vibrations of Mr Midas's body so his touch will have a transmuting effect upon other objects. And so on. It's a science fiction story, or could be made to be one.

In Wells's terms, however, it would not yet be a science-fiction story, despite the particularity of futuristic detail. Everything would depend on what happened next. And here we may return to the original legend, as Brown conveniently states it:

> Midas wishes that anything he touches henceforth shall turn into gold. The wish is granted and Midas finds that golden food is difficult to chew or digest. Wiser, he asks to have the gift taken away and is told to bathe in a certain river.

This pre-scientific legend turns on the logical twist that 'anything he touches' is to be taken literally. But the story's didactic warning against greed is moderated by its conclusion, which reintroduces the idea of supernatural benevolence. Midas has received a 'gift' (of wisdom), but it is not the one he foolishly asked for. A modern reconstruction of the whole story which eliminated the supernatural element would unquestionably be science fiction; to be good science fiction, it would probably have to eliminate Frederic

Brown's magically-endowed extraterrestrial. Yet it is the core of resemblance between the new SF story and the ancient legend which would be of prime interest to the structural theorist.

Clearly this is not a matter of 'science', but science is in any case a problematic concept, limited in time and place. In English it carries a very strong bias toward the natural sciences, so that French *science* and German *Wissenschaft* are often better translated as 'knowledge'. Darko Suvin, perhaps the most influential contemporary theoretician of SF, proposes that 'science' in this context should be replaced by the more neutral term 'cognition'; thus science fiction becomes the 'literature of cognitive estrangement'. It is 'estranged' by the introduction of some novelty which transforms the author's empirical world, and 'cognitive' by virtue of its affiliation to science and rationality. (The concept of estrangement will be further discussed in chapter 4 below.) Since the idea of cognitive estrangement assumes the dynamic interaction of its two terms, its force is clearly normative as well as descriptive. Such a definition suggests that the work in which the potentialities of science fiction are most fully realized will be that in which the 'novelty' is not only significant in itself, but is developed in the most thoroughly cognitive or scientific spirit. Cognition must be understood as embracing the polarities of the human intelligence; that is, it is at once logical and imaginative, rational and empirical, systematic and sceptical. This model of the thought-process is opposed by Suvin to the submissive and credulous attitudes of the religious or ideological believer. Thus, like many of the definitions that have been cited, the idea of cognitive estrangement takes its stand in the ongoing battle between agnostic materialism and mystical idealism. Where the genres of supernatural and heroic fantasy appeal to the 'higher' or intuitive logic of the occult, science fiction of the last two centuries, Suvin writes, is distinguished by the presence of cognition as 'the sign or correlative of a *method* . . . identical to that of a modern philosophy of science.'[18]

By extension, the criterion of proto-science fiction in

earlier periods, all the way back to the Greek legends, must be not so much its anticipation of the specific themes of later SF (such as the journey to other worlds), as its relationship to the body of cognitions in its own day. Only this can determine whether we are in the presence of a cognitive thought-experiment or an irresponsible fantasy. (The great majority of actual science fiction, it might be noted, lies somewhere between the two.) One consequence of this argument is that it becomes necessary to identify a body of what may be called anti-science fiction, the work of writers using some SF conventions but totally opposed to scientific philosophy. In the aftermath of the science-versus-religion debates of the mid-nineteenth century, a whole tradition of such anti-science fiction was produced, from Bulwer-Lytton and Marie Corelli through to A.E. Van Vogt and H.P. Lovecraft. This body of fiction remains a powerful and – many would argue – a largely pernicious force in contemporary culture; it should, of course, be sharply distinguished from the work of writers committed to a scientific or liberal-humanist world-view who occasionally dabble in occult themes. The work of C.S. Lewis, the novelist, scholar and Christian apologist, has an intellectual seriousness foreign to the Corellis and Lovecrafts, and is rightly considered to exemplify the anti-scientific position. Lewis does indeed have some cognitive insights denied to the proponents of what he calls 'scientism', but the main intention of his science-fiction trilogy is to take his readers out of the universe of modern astronomy and back to that of traditional Christianity. He was very frank about the propagandist intent of his fantasies. For this reason, readers would do well to be wary of his more strictly literary defence of mythopoeic fantasy, in his pioneering critical essay 'On Science Fiction':

> In this kind of story the pseudo-scientific apparatus is to be taken simply as a 'machine' in the sense which that word bore for the Neo-Classical critics. The most superficial appearance of plausibility – the merest sop to our critical intellect – will do. I am inclined to think that

frankly supernatural methods are best. I took a hero once to Mars in a space-ship, but when I knew better I had angels convey him to Venus. Nor need the strange worlds, when we get there, be at all strictly tied to scientific probabilities. It is their wonder, or beauty, or suggestiveness that matter.[19]

Since all modern fiction embodies an inherent world-view or metaphysic, there is no such thing as a complete innocence of wonder or fantasy. Even such a naive literature as that produced in our society for young children is ideology-laden, as recent feminist criticism has abundantly shown. Similarly, the various attempts to view science fiction as traditional mythopoeic imagination in modern dress seem to imply that the sources of creativity are ultimately mysterious and unchanging, and that these are matters before which the scientific intelligence had best stand in abeyance. Only from this point of view could the choice between taking one's hero to Mars in a space-ship or to Venus by angel-ship appear an indifferent one. Angel-transport is a characteristic device of modern Christian fantasy, but in science fiction it could only appear in a spirit of self-conscious antiquarian parody or burlesque.

Generic hybrids

The extreme narrative sophistication of some contemporary science fiction, fantasy, and postmodernist realism does, admittedly, pose problems which make the foregoing discussion appear oversimplified. While it may be true that such fiction eludes generic classification, the confusion is often deliberately contrived, and a generic approach can provide the best means of giving a critical description of the work in question. In the field of science fiction today, the relationship between theory and practice is sufficiently close for there to be a very real possibility of the novelist bringing his cognitive scepticism to bear on the definitions put forward by academic critics.

A comparison of two recent novels, Samuel Delany's *The*

Einstein Intersection (1967) and Brian Aldiss's *The Malacia Tapestry* (1976), will serve to illustrate the complexities of science-fiction genology. *The Einstein Intersection* won a Nebula Award and has been widely regarded as one of the major SF novels of the 1960s. Despite the jejune sophistication of its 'New Wave' mannerisms, this novel makes use of various readily identifiable SF conventions. It is a story of 'future history' in which alien 'psychic manifestations' from the other side of the universe have taken over the culture and bodies of human beings, who have mysteriously vanished, perhaps after a nuclear holocaust. Delany rather sketchily accounts for their disappearance in terms of Goedel's Theorem and Einstein's Theory of Relativity. These two rarefied summits of modern science are said to have had practical effects, beginning with the exploration of the known universe and ending with the migration of humanity into another continuum. So far, the story is tenable as an experiment in cognitive logic, since it may be claimed that its narrative premise is no more outlandish than the theories themselves once were. Delany's plot hinges, however, on the meaning of the human culture that the aliens have inherited. Not only do they experience this culture as a mythology, but they seem destined to live through an extraordinary assortment of mythological roles, from Christ and Orpheus to Jean Harlow, the Beatles, and Billy the Kid. Lobey, the main character, is reared in a pastoral setting where the main occupations are herding and dragon-droving. However, he is a born musician, who soon finds himself on an Orphic quest for his girl-friend Friza, who died mysteriously but returns periodically in hallucinations. His quest is a failure, but he comes back from his journey to the 'underworld' and his confrontation with Kid Death unharmed. The story's narrative development (heavily influenced by the contemporary cults of the drop-out, rock music, and LSD) clearly belong to mythopoeic fantasy.

It might be argued that such an analysis fails to acknowledge Delany's sophisticated, anthropological awareness of the functions of myth. In addition, his hero comes to believe that humanity and its inheritors are not necessarily bound by the mythical archetypes, though they must, apparently, 'exhaust the old mazes before [they] can move into the new ones'.[20] The appearance in the novel of extracts from the author's journals suggests that Lobey's entanglement in the myths of the past should be read as a projection of Delany's own search for artistic maturity. However, the level at which this parallel is established is one at which (as one of the characters remarks) 'Things passing in a world of difference have their surrealistic corollaries in the present.'[21] The meaning of *The Einstein Intersection* (which I myself would judge to be an artistic failure) must be sought among the half-realized suggestions of its fantastic world. Delany's invocation of the mythical archetype has the effect of glamourizing, rather than elucidating, his underlying allegory. Despite the superficial attractiveness of its mixture of science fiction and fantasy, Delany's novel (if this analysis is correct) has in the end the advantages of neither. In any case, the possibility of artistic failure is one of the many complicating factors in generic classification.

Difficulties of another kind are raised by Aldiss's *The Malacia Tapestry*, a novel where the reader is in no doubt of the author's mastery of his chosen material. Just as *The Einstein Intersection* appeared at first glance to observe the conventions of science fiction, Aldiss's novel seems an exercise in deliberate fantasy. Malacia is a feudal city-state in a 'parallel world' populated by astrologers, wizards, 'flighted people', satyrs and other curious fauna. The narrative focuses on the erotic exploits of two careless young gallants, Perian de Chirolo and his faithless friend Guy de Lambant. Belatedly de Chirolo comes to recognize his own selfishness and blindness to the evil around him; but this theme of moral awakening is more a narrative convenience than a source of any great insight into human experience. The result is an entertaining, quasi-historical extravaganza which was not published under the science-fiction category. Nevertheless, a case can and has been made for *The*

Malacia Tapestry as science fiction. Aldiss's imaginary world is based on a series of cognitive premises, which include an alternative process of evolution (the dinosaurs have not died out), the establishment of a 'near-utopian' city somewhere in the Byzantine empire with a regime dedicated to the preservation of stability at all costs, and – most curiously of all – an attempt to create a narrative to which the magicians and satyrs portrayed in a series of mythological drawings by G.B. Tiepolo can serve as realistic illustrations. The political situation in the fabulous city is presented in convincing detail, despite de Chirolo's heedlessness of his own ambivalent role in it. Malacia is a place of squalor and oppression, a theatre both of decadent pleasures and of class struggle. De Chirolo, by profession an underemployed actor, veers between the frivolities of the rich and a half-hearted, unstable sympathy for the people. He pursues his career as a matinée idol with the help of two new inventions (ballooning and photography) which threaten Malacia's ancestral stagnation. Eventually we realize that he is only a pawn in the ruthless struggle between the Progressives and the city's rulers. The presence of this political theme makes *The Malacia Tapestry* something very different from ordinary fantasy. (Rex Warner's political fantasies, *The Wild Goose Chase* and *The Aerodrome*, spring to mind as possible analogues). Yet, though Aldiss is a leading science-fiction writer and his novel has clear affinities with 'parallel world' SF such as Philip K. Dick's *The Man in the High Castle* or Kingsley Amis's *The Alteration*, to claim for it unquestioned science-fictional status seems somewhat extravagant. Malacia's soothsayers and 'flighted people' (cherubs) are evidence of Aldiss's predilection for a kind of whimsical, neo-Gothic fabulation which has little in common with the scientific or cognitive spirit. To attempt to account for everything in *The Malacia Tapestry* as arising from the project of an alternative historiography would be to take the political and social themes of this highly entertaining fantasia a good deal more seriously than they deserve.

It is an unfortunate result of applying a normative definition of science fiction that it is difficult to exclude a given novel without implying an adverse judgment. The catholic experimentation of a novelist like Aldiss may be more pleasing to the reader than to the puritan critic. The appearance of hybrids like *The Einstein Intersection* and *The Malacia Tapestry*, together with the revival of critical and creative interest in fantasy of all kinds which is characteristic of the later twentieth century, have led many observers to advocate the abandonment of the separate science-fiction category, or at least to prophesy its steady extinction. There are two points which may be made in reply to this. Firstly, though there are many similarities and points of contact between science fiction and the postmodernist fantasy of writers like Pynchon, Brautigan, and Lessing, similarity is not the same as identity. To take a nineteenth-century example, *Moby Dick* is a romance whose author imparts a great body of knowledge about whales and whaling with true cognitive enthusiasm; but it does not seem helpful to call it a scientific romance. Postmodernist fantasy likewise represents an adjunct rather than an addition to the genre of science fiction outlined in this chapter.

Secondly, the advantages to be gained from a gradual abandonment of SF by those equipped to write it should be questioned. Verne's and Heinlein's 'future realism', however limiting it may now seen, gave popular expression to a genuine imaginative excitement about technological and scientific possibilities, and it was widely read with a sense of exhilaration and discovery. The recent discussion of 'speculative fiction' is, from one point of view, symptomatic of mid-twentieth-century disillusionment with scientific prospects. Our civilization is founded on scientific and cognitive attitudes, so that the issues raised by the science fiction/fantasy distinction ultimately involve the survival and continued advance of humanity as a whole. These are cataclysmal realities which dwarf the day-by-day concerns of the literary analyst of cataclysmal fantasies. Nevertheless, a world in which there was no longer a branch of writing giving special expression to the scientific and cognitive reaches of the imagination would be a different and, in all probability, a much grimmer world than the one in which we live. The mere act of imagining such a world and how it might come about is a rudimentary form of science fiction.

2 THE SOCIOLOGY OF THE GENRE

SCIENCE fiction, in many obvious and not-so-obvious ways, reflects the nature of modern society. A serious and wide-ranging critical treatment of this literary form would be virtually impossible without some consideration of its sociology. The sociologist may approach an SF story in one of three ways: as a *product*, bearing the imprint of social forces at every level from fundamental narrative structures to the precise forms in which it is manufactured, distributed and sold; as a communication or *message*, with a particular function for a particular audience; and, finally, as a *document* articulating and passing judgment upon the social situation from which it emerges. The considerations involved in seeing science fiction or any other cultural form as product, message, and document are so diverse that it may be misleading to bring them under a single heading. In addition, the separation between 'critical' and 'sociological' approaches to literary material is often artificial. The level at which SF texts exist as documents, for instance, is not easily distinguishable from their role as social criticism (to be discussed in chapter 4). What characterizes the sociological approach to science fiction in the long run is that it is concerned to set the individual genre within the total social process to which it belongs.

A simple way of relating a given body of texts to society as a whole is to isolate some element of literary content, which may then be discussed as a phenomenon in its own right. For example, we can learn (or have the illusion of learning) about the social 'image' of scientists or computer engineers by examining their portrayal in a range of SF texts. A second approach is to find out who reads these texts – for whom, that is, do the 'images' purveyed in science fiction serve as a message?[1] The information provided by readership surveys is useful not only to publishers and advertisers, but to the sociologist concerned with the meaning of SF as a cultural phenomenon. Yet there is a major drawback to the content-analyses and readership surveys which constituted a large proportion of the early sociology of popular literature. Their results can only be interpreted on the basis of certain implicit assumptions about the workings of the texts concerned and their place in general social life. It is these assumptions which the more recent varieties of literary sociology have set out to formulate and question. Sociological critics now undertake to distinguish between the manifest content of SF, and the latent causes and significance of the imaginative structures it employs; they ask not only who reads it, but how and why it is read; and, finally, they are prepared to consider it, not merely as a mirror, but as a source of active commentary upon society and its attitudes.

SF as product

Literature considered as a product may be attributed either to society as a whole, or to a particular class or group or cultural force within it. The first of these alternatives is exemplified by the observation that SF usually flourishes only in highly industrialized societies. A necessary extension leads to the separate analysis of the various national traditions of the genre; thus, as a first crude approximation, Russian science fiction is seen to have been conditioned by its response to (and, at times, criticism of) the official utopianism of the Soviet state; British science fiction owes its repeated visions of catastrophe to the long national history of industrial and imperial decline; German science fiction is replete with visions of the triumph of a master race; and American science fiction derives both the optimism and the ruthlessness of its approach from the frontier experience and the economic subjugation of the West. There has as yet been rather little progress towards such a comparative sociology,[2] partly because of the overwhelming influence of American science fiction in the period 1930–60 (this itself, of course, is something that requires explanation), and partly because of the political internationalism that SF writers and the scientific community normally profess. Science fiction, however, can be described as a homogeneous, international literature only to the extent that one is prepared to accept the conventional American view of it – as reflected, for example, in an anthology title like *The Best From the Rest of the World* – and to ignore local differences.

One of the commonest forms taken by the internationalist view of science fiction is that of critics who regard it as the inevitable and necessary expression of the contemporary 'human condition'. Thus – to give three somewhat diverse examples – Robert Scholes views it as the literature of the Darwinian and Einsteinian revolution which has 'replaced Historical Man with Structural Man'.[3] Alvin Toffler suggests that its function is to help its readers adjust to 'future shock', or the constantly accelerating pace of social and technological change.[4] And Scott Sanders argues that science fiction's tendency to present a de-individualized world of robots, androids, and featureless human beings results not from its artistic inadequacies but from its grasp of the phenomena of twentieth-century alienation.[5] In each case, the critics are seeking to reduce the complexity of life today to a single existential formula. It may be added that theories like these are by no means as strictly sociological as they claim to be. Their real intention is presumably that of altering the ways in which science fiction is read and understood.

Alienation and 'future shock' are, of course, real aspects of the contemporary world in which science fiction is produced and on which it reflects. Yet the multiplicity of available sociological and social-psychological descriptions of the 'contemporary world' is itself a cultural phenomenon of our times. Evidently it satisfies some deeply-felt need in the modern intellectual to be told that he is the victim of a 'runaway world', of the 'affluent society', of the 'culture of narcissism', or of a number of other social diseases. Science fiction can be made to provide evidence for any or all of these diagnoses. If we look for the underlying political and economic processes which have given rise to the contemporary sense of malaise and victimization, then SF must be seen as one among the many products of the later stages of capitalism, or of Western imperialism, or of industrialization.

In fact, the strange new worlds of science fiction very often present a distorted and yet recognizable image of capitalism, imperialism or industrialization. Marc Angenot has argued that the basis of Jules Verne's series of *voyages extraordinaires* is a liberal-capitalist utopia of free circulation.[6] Fantasies of galactic conquest undoubtedly contain a form of transferred imperialism (see chapter 4). Raymond Williams devotes a section of *The Country and the City* (1973) to discussing science fiction as a response to the 'crisis of metropolitan experience' brought about by industrialization (pp. 272-8). The spread of cities gives rise to the vision of 'human ecology', or of the total planning and control of man's environment; such an environment is then condemned in anti-utopian SF as being, in a fundamental sense, 'dehumanized'. Williams's essay is a highly illuminating attempt to see science fiction as one among the many symptoms of a developing social pathology. Yet we are still some way from identifying the specific determinants of the genre as we know it.

In the terms proposed by Lucien Goldmann's influential work on French neoclassical drama,[7] those determinants would have to be found in the existence of a social class whose outlook or world-view SF expresses. And, it would seem, there is such a class, whose rise closely parallels the rise of the science-fiction genre. The word 'scientist' was coined in 1840. Large numbers of scientific journals, societies, and laboratories were founded in the mid-Victorian decades, and one of the first beneficiaries of the spread of scientific education was H.G. Wells. Since Wells's time, the links between SF and the outlook of scientists and technologists have remained fairly close. Many scientists have written SF; the genre has been reviewed and discussed from time to time in scientific journals; and some of its professional writers have also been best-selling scientific popularizers or have held office in such organizations as the British Interplanetary Society. Magazine SF has undoubtedly helped to spread a scientific ideology among its juvenile readers and to recruit them into the scientific and technical professions. There is enough evidence here to suggest that the historians and sociologists of twentieth-century science might do well to consider the influence of science fiction on their chosen subjects.

I have argued elsewhere that modern science fiction has evolved as a developing response to what may be called the scientific world-view.[8] May we, then, look upon the genre as a product of the collective consciousness of a particular social class? The definition of a social 'class' is, of course, controversial; certainly the Wellsian dream that the élite of scientists and technologists might become a self-conscious political force capable of seizing power from the established rulers has not been realized in any country. A very confident Goldmannesque analysis of science fiction has recently been put forward by Gérard Klein, who claims to identify the 'precise characteristics' of the 'scientifically and technologically oriented middle class' whose consciousness 'delimits' American SF.[9] Klein attributes the transition in American SF from early twentieth-century optimism to subsequent pessimism to the rise and decline of the expectations and status of the scientific middle class. The evidence, however, is inevitably somewhat circular. Those who managed to articulate the consciousness of the class to which Klein refers were – almost invariably – science-fiction writers, while the other most palpable members of the 'class' were their readers and fans. At the present time Klein's thesis is not so much a sociology as a powerful literary idea which enables him to divide science fiction into periods and to suggest that there are good socio-economic reasons for its present state of pessimism and 'discontent'. Much more work needs to be done to substantiate what one suspects is a fairly complex relationship between science fiction and the actual shifts in the collective experience and outlook of scientific workers.

One of the merits of Klein's argument is that it takes account of the dramatic growth in the readership for science fiction since 1960. 'For the first time in its history,' he states, 'SF is aware that it speaks in the name of a very great number of people, and is understood by them.'[10] His explanation for this is that the possessors of scientific and technological training are no longer a small élite but a growing sector of a middle class which has itself lost much of its former prestige and independence. Post-1960 SF responds to the era of multinational corporations with its vision of a neo-feudal world in which the individual is condemned to servitude. Such visions reflect the apprehensions and fears of an ever-broadening social group in today's society. There can, of course, be no empirical proof that readers turn to the genre for these reasons; indeed, it seems possible that Klein would dismiss their own attempts to rationalize their literary preferences as being subjective and irrelevant. Klein's essay, though far too brief and speculative to be wholly persuasive, suggests one of the main directions that the sociology of SF might be – and, up to now, has not been – taking.

SF as message: readership and 'fandom'

Traditionally, the readers of science fiction were more than 90 per cent male, and a majority were scientists and technicians. Today a substantial extension of the readership has taken place, most notably among women and among college students and graduates in the humanities and social sciences. The recent spate of anthologies of feminist SF, and the creation of a kind of science-fiction 'campus-novel' by writers such as Roger Zelazny and John Boyd, suggest the special efforts which are being made to cater to these two groups. Nevertheless, the broad socio-economic profile of SF readers and fans has apparently remained unchanged in many respects. John W. Campbell claimed as a result of a 1958 readership survey in *Astounding* that his readers were much better educated than the national average, and that a large proportion of them were 'decision-influencing executives in major manufacturing industries'.[11] While this was no doubt an inflated boast, recent surveys confirm the existence of generally high levels of educational attainment and job satisfaction among SF fans. Not only are they heavily involved in professional and technical employment, but they claim to experience a degree of freedom and independence at work which suggest their 'identification with and aspiration to positions of high status within their society'.[12] In terms of the broad categories used here, it would seem that while SF has greatly increased its readership, it has not necessarily done so by appealing to a fundamentally different type of reader. The changes in the readership are most probably explained by the extension and dilution of what Klein calls the 'scientifically and technologically oriented middle class' of earlier decades.

Various qualifications should be made to this. SF fans are not the same as SF readers, and it is the self-selected group of fans who travel to conventions whose socio-economic characteristics have recently been studied in depth. Attendance at fan conventions is a phenomenon peculiar to science fiction, which demands assessment in any sociological account of the genre. Unlike all other modes of popular fiction, SF has since the 1930s attracted to itself the trappings of an organized (and predominantly youthful) subculture.[13] It is not necessary to describe the inveterate institutions of fandom – the cyclostyled 'fanzines', the raucous get-togethers, the flamboyant repertoire of private acronyms – in this context. Nor is this the place to consider the effect of fandom on SF writers, though it is acknowledged to have served both as a very effective source of new talent, and as the medium of a level of dialogue between authors and readers unknown in other departments of fiction. Instead, the following question will be put: why did organized fandom come into existence in science fiction, and not in other, apparently comparable modes of popular expression?

Science fiction, I would argue, has given rise to a sub-culture because it promotes a shared view of reality towards which the rest of society is felt to be significantly hostile or indifferent. Organized fandom is a mode of retaliation against that indifference. For the most part, such retaliation simply takes the form of collective self-assertion by a group who feel themselves to be bound together by experience, interests, and, to a lesser extent, by age. However, it also has political and cultural implications which cannot be over-looked. To adopt the terminology of the 1960s, SF is a mode of counter-culture, propagating visions and conceptions of altered modes of life which would normally be ridiculed or dismissed by the representatives of orthodoxy. In other words, it serves to promote exploratory thinking and im-agining outside the limits of established social conventions. Only their addiction to the excitement of such thinking and imagining can account for the energy and enthusiasm lavished on the genre by its fans. Though George Orwell's boyhood belongs to an earlier epoch, his description of his early discovery of H.G. Wells remains true to some aspects of the fans' experience to this day:

> Back in the nineteen-hundreds it was a wonderful experience for a boy to discover H.G. Wells. There you were, in a world of pedants, clergymen and golfers, with your future employers exhorting you to 'get on or get out', your parents systematically warping your sexual life, and your dull-witted schoolmasters sniggering over their Latin tags; and here was this wonderful man who could tell you about the inhabitants of the planets and the bottom of the sea, and who *knew* that the future was not going to be what respectable people imagined. ('Wells, Hitler and the World State')

The fantasies shared by SF readers are, unquestionably, fantasies of liberation such as those experienced by Orwell. However, this is not to say that the fans are notably radical or revolutionary in their social attitudes. They show few signs either of political activity or of affiliation with middle-class protest movements such as the anti-nuclear campaign or the student movement of the late 1960s. The most that one can point to is a widespread, though often very partial, awareness of science fiction among the proponents of alternative and 'counter-cultural' lifestyles in the last two decades. (One extreme of this was the adoption of Heinlein's *Stranger in a Strange Land* as a near-sacred text by Ken Kesey and Charles Manson and their respective groups of followers.) The fans, however, remain a very different group from those who might profess a nodding acquaintance with Le Guin's *The Left Hand of Darkness*, say, or Herbert's *Dune*. It seems quite likely that science fiction acts not only to propagate dreams of liberation, but to sublimate the anxieties of those who fear the impermanence of the status quo rather than its repressiveness. Thus a sub-culture like that of the fans can well span differences in temperament between the radical and the conservative, the zealot and the dilettante. What holds them together, besides a mere habit of reading, is a shared vision of possibilities which only those within the circle of initiates seem to comprehend or take seriously.

Modes of reading

In discussing fandom, we have moved inevitably from considering science fiction as a product to considering it as a message. No simple theory of social determinism can account for the formation of a sub-culture, which presupposes an active response among self-selected groups of people to meanings found in the culture around them. In the case of SF these meanings are found through the medium of a commodity which is manufactured, marketed, and bought in very similar ways to other kinds of popular fiction. Not surprisingly, it is more often included than excluded from generalizations about the literary 'mass media'. Like other highly commercialized forms of writing,

SF has been dismissed innumerable times as lowbrow, semi-literate, ephemeral, and trashy. Even where it is granted some degree of superiority among popular literary forms, this has often been on intellectual or social grounds (such as its 'idea' content and its appeal to a fairly educated readership) rather than because it is allowed to have any standing as 'literature'.

Any sustained acquaintance with science fiction will dispel the notion that it is all composed of popular trash. Those who regard it as trash are merely ignorant. Nevertheless, the sociology of literature is properly concerned with the large proportion (in SF, following Theodore Sturgeon, this is conventionally put at 90 per cent) of the total literary output which is barely competent – or worse. What are the effects, it may be asked, of the 'indiscriminate' reading of science fiction? As with television, comic strips, pornography, and other media of which this question is put, the answer depends very much on the kinds of use that the audience makes of it. Does the idea of 'light reading', for example, imply a capacity to detach oneself from the material, to remain fundamentally unaffected by it, that is not present in the case of 'serious' reading? The question illustrates how much, in the terminology of reading, we normally take for granted. For it seems likely that, at all levels of literacy, personal needs play as large a part in determining the degree of attention that we are prepared to bring to a particular textual encounter as does the nature of the text itself. At the sociological level, it is possible to distinguish between various different modes of reading, which any literate person can draw upon. There is, however, no *necessary* connection between any of the modes of reading and a particular kind of work. The morning newspaper can be read as meticulously as the Calvinist reads his Bible. Nevertheless, every written text carries with it a cultural context (both internal and external to the work itself) which contains strong suggestions as to the mode of reading that is appropriate. In science fiction, the phenomenon of fandom both arises out of, and contributes to, this cultural context.

All literacy is formed within a particular historical tradition. In Western civilization, the ultimate source for this is the invention of the alphabet, with its resources of simplicity, flexibility, and scope for individual expression. It is, however, only in the last three hundred years that popular literacy has become widespread, above all in the Protestant countries where the use of books for everyday devotional purposes was already common in the seventeenth century. The various stages of the industrial revolution have brought a vast increase in the quantity of fictions capable of impinging on the daily life of the average citizen, until, in the later twentieth century, television, radio, newspapers, magazines, paperbacks, song lyrics, and advertisement hoardings bombard him with the materials of fantasy at every turn.

In ordinary British and American pre-industrial homes it may be assumed that, where reading took place at all, it was largely repetitive. A few books, such as the Bible, Shakespeare, or *The Pilgrim's Progress*, would be read again and again, either by the same person or by various members of the family.* Often reading was a communal experience, orally shared and passed down from one generation to the next. The impression given by this is one of cultural stability, but in fact wherever books have been available they have served as an inducement to accumulative reading – reading, that is, whose purpose is the deliberate acquisition of knowledge, either for its own sake or as a means of obtaining social advancement. Accumulative reading, such as a student pursues through school and university, normally involves the absorption of a continually increasing supply of books, though in the beginning these might be very few. Societies possessing the economic means to develop a large

---

* The BBC radio programme 'Desert Island Discs', in which it is assumed that the castaway would inevitably wish to have the Bible and Shakespeare with him (or her) on the island, is a throwback to this situation. For most of the celebrities interviewed, the choice of a third book to take with them (the *Oxford Book of English Verse*? a collection of jokes? crossword puzzles or seafood recipes? a really long novel?) is an audible source of embarrassment.

supply of books, however, are likely to cater for a third kind of reading, that of the habitual consumer who becomes accustomed to perusing large numbers of broadly similar works. Such habitual reading begins in urban societies (if only because of the availability of leisure and the economics of distribution) and is practised at all levels of society including the intelligentsia. Characteristic of modern 'light reading' is the disposability of the materials involved; they are not filed away for future reference or re-reading but returned to the library, traded or thrown away.[14] Specialized magazine fiction, sold at newspaper counters, produced on pulp paper which will not stand up to much wear and tear, and invariably offered in plural quantities (*True Confessions, True Romances, Amazing Stories*), is aimed both to satisfy and perpetuate the demand for fiction that can be regularly consumed and disposed of – a demand which in modern society begins as soon as the 'reading habit' is acquired by children, and which might almost be said to define that habit.

Finally, what of 'critical reading', the mode of literary response taught in schools and universities which has as its end-product a more or less articulate appraisal of the work in question? It may be doubted whether this is really a separable mode of reading at all. The skills that it calls for involve, rather, a combination of the types of reading already mentioned – the resilience of the habitual consumer, the dogged determination of the seeker after knowledge, and, not least, the patient and reverent scrutiny of the devotee. 'Critical reading' differs in that the end-product is different: the framing of a judgment, which is itself very often a mode of literary composition (even if it is expressed in nothing more elaborate than a 'sentence' or aphorism). The teaching of literature cannot directly impart any of the techniques of reading – it can only exemplify the manner in which a sophisticated reader would use them. What it does impart is the technique of analysing and assessing what the reader experiences in a given text.

Turning back to science fiction, it is clear that a large

proportion of the reading of this genre is of the order of habitual consumption. Nevertheless, the evidence suggests that SF consumers are more discriminating than are the consumers of some of the other popular genres. This point was argued in a 1976 article in *Publishers' Weekly* by the chief buyer for a large American bookselling chain:

> SF customers are author oriented. They have their favorites and shop for those first. They do not shop first by type, unlike a pattern found in romances where the customers buy Regency period novels, in male adventure where they buy spy novels or mercenary novels, and in westerns where they buy super violence rather than more traditional historical westerns.[15]

Once again, the touchstone for understanding the reading of SF would seem to be the institution of fandom, even though only a tiny minority of the 'customers' referred to above are active fans. Fandom, however indiscriminate it might appear to an outsider, is incompatible with simple reading for consumption. SF fans go beyond the simple entertainment motive by turning their favoured reading into something between a cult and a field of knowledge. Cultism leads to the intensive sharing of reading experiences among groups of friends and associates and, at its furthest extreme, to the elevation of certain books such as *Stranger in a Strange Land* to a semi-scriptural status. SF novels normally only enter the best-selling list when they acquire a cult reputation of this kind.

The true SF fan, however, is distinguished by his breadth of reading in the genre rather than by his passionate allegiance to any particular author or text. (Fantasy readers, by contrast, very rarely go beyond cultism to become fans in the science-fictional sense.) Becoming a fan involves initiation into an unofficial field of knowledge, which, on inspection, has various parallels with the official field of orthodox literary knowledge. Science fiction has its acknowledged ancestors – named by Gernsback as Poe, Wells, and Verne – and its own contemporary 'classics' and 'traditions'.

The desire (at least) to recognize literary quality was shown by the institution in 1953 of the Hugo Award, granted to the best novel of the year as decided by fans at the World Science Fiction Convention. The paperback production of SF, which also began in the early 1950s, has enabled publishers to promote the whole *oeuvres* of selected popular authors, and to exercise control over which of their works have remained in print in the ensuing decades. At the same time, the existence of fandom ensures that the contents of the 'science-fiction shelf' in library or bookstore are never quite the same as the canon known to the initiated. Fandom maintains a 'folk-memory', based in part upon repetitive and accumulative reading, and manifesting itself through a system of personal recommendation and exchange which is quite separate from the publicity and distribution techniques of the commercial market. Connoisseurship is born as a proportion of readers do not throw away the 'disposable' magazines and paperbacks, but hoard, collect and re-read them. Finally, fans begin to write critically about their reading and to circulate such writing in the form of 'fanzines'.

The significance of these developments is that, long before science fiction came to be studied in universities, it had given rise to all the modes of reading which may be brought to bear on high literature. Yet these were mediated through the unofficial, alternative institutions of what is now known as the 'SF ghetto'. As the latter term indicates, it is not necessarily wrong to look upon the fans as victims of cultural impoverishment. Nevertheless, their activities constitute a vital response to and reaction against such impoverishment. And, as Linda Fleming writes of American SF, 'The literature and the subculture have evolved together, each shaping characteristics of the other.'[16]

SF as document: the 'thinking machine'

As yet little has been said of the actual value that run-of-the-mill science fiction may have for its devotees. This ques-

tion cannot be discussed in the terms of conventional literary criticism, and as yet few adequate answers have been
given to it. The seriousness with which SF fans regard their
chosen pursuit suggests that they see it not merely as a
diversion but as a mode of knowledge – and of knowledge,
moreover, towards which the rest of society is hostile or
indifferent. In many cases the knowledge offered by science
fiction takes the tangible form of ideas; the genre has been
widely regarded as a 'literature of ideas', especially political
and scientific ones. Often these ideas are in advance of their
time, and sometimes the speculative form of science fiction
has enabled them to avoid the censorship they would otherwise attract. The earliest story dealing with atomic weapons,
for example, is Wells's *The World Set Free* (1913), and one of
its many successors – 'Deadline', by Cleve Cartmill – drew
the attention of US military intelligence when it was published in *Astounding Science Fiction* in 1944. The intelligence
agents who arrived at the offices of *Astounding* assumed that
the story must constitute evidence of a security leak. Within
the SF field, however, this was an absurd assumption;
atomic fission and its consequences had been subjects of
speculation for years, and if writers in *Astounding* could not
keep ahead of what was public knowledge in weapons technology, what would be the point in reading them? Editor
John W. Campbell argued that the sudden disappearance of
nuclear-energy stories from his magazine would, rightly, be
regarded as suspicious.

The magazines of this period also served at times to anticipate matters of social and political debate and even,
during the McCarthy years in America, to voice embattled
liberal attitudes which could hardly get a hearing elsewhere.
In a pioneering article on 'The Cold War in Science Fiction',
T.A. Shippey has demonstrated the regularity with which,
during these years, stories in *Astounding* offered their
readers a sophisticated understanding of the problems
involved in top-secret research and its relation to govern-
mental control.[17] He suggests that the fantastic elements of
many SF stories served as 'a cover, or a frame, for discussion

of many real issues which were hardly open to serious consideration in any other popular medium: issues such as the nature of science, the conflict of business and government, the limits of loyalty, the power of social norms to affect individual perception'. Science fiction was acting as a ' "thinking machine" for the convenience of people largely without academic support or intellectual patronage'.[18] Despite the general lifting of political and ideological restrictions on free discussion since the 1950s, SF has continued to act in much the way that Shippey describes. The influence of certain of its writers and books on groups such as ecologists and women's liberationists is well known. Less visible, perhaps, is the extent to which SF has continued to influence the opinions and attitudes of a large number of young and more or less uncommitted members of every generation of post-Second World War adults.

Literature and paraliterature

In his book, *Adventure, Mystery, and Romance* (1976), John G. Cawelti argues that popular fiction is distinguished by its formulaic quality. The question whether science fiction is, indeed, formulaic will be pursued in the next chapter. At this point we may note that the idea of formula fiction is necessarily at variance with that of run-of-the-mill SF as a 'thinking machine'. The one views fiction as a message beamed at a largely passive audience, while the other sees it as a document embodying significant reflections upon the society which produced it. Cawelti suggests that there are four typical modes of relationship between the fiction that he discusses – notably thrillers, westerns, and best-selling melodramas – and society as a whole. Such fiction may tend either to confirm conventional attitudes, to bring about a resolution of social tensions and ambiguities, to embark upon a controlled exploration of 'forbidden' territory, or to promote cultural continuity in the form of reconciliation between the new and the old.[19] There is no place in this scheme for a literature of genuine innovation, or for one of informal 'underground' education and enlightenment such as SF aspires to be. The whole notion of a literature of ideas suggests a reader who, far from being invisibly manipulated, may be provoked into arriving at his own assessment of the arguments contained within the story. Fiction which has this effect cannot be viewed as merely diverting the audience with well-proven formulas or as exploiting its readers' 'inferior training and lower imaginative capacity'.[20] Here we are not confronted by a 'mass medium' effect but by literature which makes a rather special appeal to a self-selected audience. Nevertheless, science fiction is a popular form, and not (as some might have it) a mode of high literature which the critical establishment has, until the present, unaccountably overlooked.

The process by which a small proportion of texts once condemned as trivial and vulgar find their way into the approved tradition is a familiar one in literary history. The rise of the novel itself is the most celebrated example. It is, thus, quite wrong to assume that popular literature is invariably characterized by the poverty and uninventiveness of the reading experiences it offers. Frequently it can communicate with its readers as richly and variously as the 'high literature' contemporary with it – but its richness is unacknowledged and unofficial, since it is not part of the self-consciousness of literary culture.

What we call literary culture can, of course, only exist on a basis of inclusion and exclusion. Yet, sociologically speaking, it cannot be seen as an impartial custodian of values since it has a strong interest in asserting and preserving its own identity. Hence its tendency to show tolerance towards mediocrity within its own ranks (the 'immature' or 'amateurish' play or poem, the 'failed' works of an otherwise distinguished author), and merciless hostility towards real and imagined mediocrity outside it. The consensus judgments of literary criticism at any one time are less remarkable for their accuracy than for the authority vested within them. The position of popular literature (or, to use the more neutral term preferred by recent investigators, 'paraliterature') in regard to high literature is not so much one of inferiority as of *marginality*. This idea has been formulated by Marc Angenot, in a study of *Le roman populaire* (1975), as follows:

> Paraliterature occupies the space outside the literary enclosure, as a forbidden, taboo, and perhaps degraded product – held at bay, and yet rich in themes and obsessions which are repressed in high culture.[21]

Paraliterature, then, is not the lowest kind of literature in qualitative terms (there are many more bad sonnets written each year than bad SF novels), but, rather, literature's dialectical opposite. 'Literature' cannot exist as a self-contained system without this bearer of the latent dreams, aspirations, and perceptions which it excludes.

In Angenot's account, paraliterature is a product of the industrial age, beginning with urban broadsheets, 'Newgate calendars' and the Gothic novel. (On a broader interpretation, however, demotic and plebeian modes of writing, including some of the earliest science-fiction texts, are as old as literature itself.)[22] *Le roman populaire* undertakes to extend the analysis of fictional forms put forward by Lucien Goldmann in *Pour une sociologie du roman* (1964), arguing that the nineteenth-century popular romance should be seen as the dialectical opposite of the classical realist novel as Goldmann defined it. Where Balzac and Stendhal present the ironic narrative of an alienated hero searching for values in a degraded society, the romance beginning with Eugène Sue takes shape as the celebration of a Promethean hero searching for values in a regenerate society.[23] This does not make the romance any more 'liberated' than its realistic counterpart, since it is helpless in the face of the pervasive ambiguity and false consciousness in modern society, which the realistic novel attempts to master through irony. Angenot does not extend his purview to the twentieth-century novel. Nevertheless, his book serves as a provocative reminder that apparently mass-produced and commercialized modes of fiction are often the vehicles for deep-seated aspirations and needs which the high literature of the same period denies or ignores. The exact paraliterary role of science fiction at its various stages of development has still to be defined. What is clear, however, is that if we wish to understand this genre we must consider it, not as a formulaic 'subliterature', but as an autonomous mode of writing with a history and traditions at variance with, and partly suppressed by, the dominant literary forms.

As is evident from this all-too-brief summary, the detailed 'sociology of the novel' as practised by Goldmann, in his later work, and by Angenot, centres on the nature of the hero and the nineteenth-century opposition between romance and realism. Thus literary sociology turns into a form of genre criticism. One of the most obvious features of popular fiction today is that much of it continues to celebrate the deeds of 'men of action' long after the values of individual prowess have been discredited at the highest levels of literary realism. It is possible to see here a thwarted refusal, on the part of popular authors, to capitulate to the obsession with the limitations and uncertainties of modern life which preoccupies the realists. At the same time, the portrayal of triumphant, 'superhuman' individualism in a modern context argues a certain wilful blindness to reality. Such blindness may keep alive a vision of larger possibilities, but it may also represent the unthinking repetition of formulas and stereotypes from the literary past. These stereotypes serve to console the reader and to reinforce his acceptance of present-day limitations. It follows that the necessary distinctions between commercialized 'formula fiction' and the potentially subversive mode of 'paraliterature' can only be made with reference to particular texts and groups of texts, and by the methods of literary criticism. The next chapter will explore various contemporary versions of the concept of narrative formulas, grouping them, however, under the heading of the traditional genre most consistently associated with ideas of pattern and repetition. The sociological study of science fiction as popular literature shades over almost inevitably into the consideration of it as a mode of romance.

3 SCIENCE FICTION AS ROMANCE

T WO things may be said immediately about the romance: it has an old and honoured place in literary history, and it spans the division between literature and paraliterature that was introduced in the previous chapter. The intrinsic popularity of romance influences almost every critical judgment that is made upon this branch of writing. Contemporary romances have in most ages been viewed with a certain contempt. Pleasing but not instructive, *dulce* but not *utile*, they have been targets of moral disapproval from the time of Plato to that of the modern realist who condemns them as anti-rational and anti-scientific. Romance also has its defenders, for whom the claims of this 'irresponsible' and 'escapist' form are the claims of the creative imagination itself. 'Nature never set forth the earth in so rich tapestry as divers poets have done. . . . Her world is brazen, the poets only deliver a golden', as Sidney wrote. Today, it is easy to point to the romances of previous ages, from *A Midsummer Night's Dream* to *Kubla Khan*, which are now enshrined in the literary tradition. Yet these cases are a small minority. The vast majority of romances belong to paraliterature, and always have done.

Critics who regard realistic novels as the normative form of prose narrative tend to define the romance in terms of its difference from realism. Thus Richard Chase in *The American Novel and Its Tradition* (1957) describes it as a sort of 'non-novel':

... the romance ... feels free to render reality in less volume and detail. It tends to prefer action to character, and action will be freer in a romance than in a novel, encountering, as it were, less resistance from reality. ... Human beings will on the whole be shown in ideal relation – that is, they will share emotions only after these have become abstract or symbolic. ... Being less committed to the immediate rendition of reality than the novel, the romance will more freely veer toward mythic, allegorical, and symbolistic forms.[1]

An alternative approach, deriving from the 'myth-critics' of the 1940s and 1950s, sees romance not as a deviation from realism but as a more fundamental and universal narrative mode. Romance, on this anthropological view, is the great mediator between primitive myth and the later and more specialized forms of fictional discourse such as realism and satire. Northrop Frye's theory of literary modes, though highly controversial, has influenced almost every subsequent treatment of the subject. Frye believes that all literature may be seen as 'a complication of a relatively restricted and simple group of formulas that can be studied in primitive culture'.[2] In romance, these formulas, derived from the rhythms of human fertility and mortality and of the seasons, remain closer to the narrative surface than in realism. In the course of his exposition of the formulas in his *Anatomy of Criticism* (1957), Frye describes science fiction as 'a mode of romance with a strong inherent tendency to myth'.[3]

Frye's formal definition of romance is clearly intended to suggest the pervasive structural influence of folk-tales and fairy-tales in the subsequent history of narrative:

If superior in *degree* to other men and to the environment, the hero is the typical hero of *romance*, whose actions are marvellous but who is himself identified as a human being. The hero of romance moves in a world in which the ordinary laws of nature are slightly suspended: prodigies of courage and endurance, unnatural to us, are natural to him, and enchanted weapons, talking animals, terrifying ogres and witches, and talismans of miraculous power violate no rule of probability once the postulates of romance have been established.[4]

The modern writing at which this definition points is of two kinds. First of all there is the deliberately archaic mode now known as heroic fantasy. William Morris, J.R.R. Tolkien and other writers who have taken the Arthurian legends, the sagas or other early literature as their models produce a kind of narrative which is literally very close to Frye's description. More generally, however, the ordinary laws of nature are slightly suspended in a much wider range of popular fiction, in which the settings are quite different from those that Frye evokes. Thus westerns, thrillers, historical novels, and the exploits of heroes such as Tarzan and James Bond can all be included under the heading of contemporary romance. The ordinary laws of human nature are also suspended to some degree in the erotic romance, a category which Frye's definition unexpectedly overlooks. (In the present-day book-trade, it may be remembered, the 'romance' label is entirely confined to stories of amorous passion. It would, however, take a much more extensive survey than can be offered here to trace the connections between the various academic definitions of the romance genre and the use of the term in everyday speech.)

If westerns, thrillers, historical novels, and love-stories all come under the heading of romance, does not science fiction do so too? The question might be asked another way: at what point does the 'romance' label become so broad that it loses all real meaning? For in the great majority of realistic novels, and not merely in SF, the laws of nature are slightly suspended. We do not call realistic novels romances since, along with the formulas and archetypes of interest to the myth-critic, they contain within them a great deal that is antagonistic to romance. The same is true of science fiction, at least to the extent that its speculations profess an ultimate loyalty to logic, probability, and the cognitive intelligence.

In *The Romance* (1970), Gillian Beer argues that romance is an 'essentially subjective' literary form, presenting an absorbing, coherent, and yet arbitrary vision of the world, which the reader can only enter at the price of a willing surrender to the writer's authority.[5] Once again, there is a sense in which this is true of all fiction. In realism, however, the fundamental arbitrariness of fictional invention is cloaked in the illusion of verisimilitude. The narrator tells the story in such a way as to produce the sustained conviction that these things might really have happened. In twentieth-century 'high literature' there has been a growing tendency to disrupt the realistic illusion, either by deliberately reintroducing an element of atavistic fantasy (as in many of D.H. Lawrence's tales), or by the cultivation of narrative self-consciousness. The masterpieces of 'post-realistic' fiction such as Joyce's *Ulysses* have made it much easier to think of all fiction as a multi-levelled construction, which achieves its distinctive identity by the combination of elements that it adds to the basic arbitrariness and subjectivity of the decision to tell a made-up story. Those elements or devices commonly associated with SF include the provision of a rational or quasi-scientific explanation of the fictive events, the projection of a future or alternative history, social criticism, and a style which asserts either the factuality or, at least, the logical admissibility of the story that is told. If the romance-writer often takes pride in the sheer arbitrariness of his fictions, SF does its best to hide that arbitrariness with the mask of necessity.

Contemporary mythology and the 'literature of wonder'

One of the main reasons for describing science fiction as a form of romance is that its subject-matter is romantic: in Shelley's words, it is not concerned with 'ordinary relations of existing events'. Modern SF has done its best to convey the sheer excitement (and horror) of the vistas opened up by science and technology. Like its literary predecessor, the 'marvellous voyage', it has often set out to amaze and astound its readers. But if wonder is the authentic response to much science fiction, it is also a very wide spread mode of literary experience. There is, no doubt, something science-fictional in Miranda's exclamation in *The Tempest*:

> O, wonder!
> How many goodly creatures are there here!
> How beauteous mankind is! O brave new world
> That has such people in't!

But the same cannot be said for the pure whimsy evoked by Donne's question in 'The Good-Morrow': 'I wonder, by my troth, what thou and I /Did, till we lov'd?' and, as any number of poets have reminded us, wonder is also to be found throughout the everyday world. The possible grounds of wonder are infinite, and wonder is always changing. T.E. Hulme wrote that it 'can only be the attitude of a man passing from one stage to another, it can never be a permanently fixed thing'.[6] Thus the idea that science fiction might be adequately described as a 'literature of wonder' should be regarded with suspicion.[7] The great pitfall of the self-conscious modern romance is that it is obliged to recreate the effect of wonder over and over again. This is why romance-writers such as Stevenson seek to induce a child-like state in the reader, since it is in childhood that we most readily surrender to the emotions of rapture:

> In anything fit to be called the name of reading . . . we should gloat over a book, be rapt clean out of ourselves, and rise from the perusal, our mind filled with the busiest, kaleidoscopic dance of images, incapable of sleep or of continuous thought. The words, if the book be eloquent, should run thenceforward in our ears like the noise of breakers, and the story, if it be a story, repeat itself in a thousand coloured pictures to the eye. (R.L. Stevenson, 'A Gossip on Romance')

In the case of modern adult readers it seems likely that only the utmost skills of the literary artist could product effects like these. They are certainly not inherent in the writer's subject-matter, whether this consists of the futuristic excitement of science fiction, or the 'ideal and timeless' elements of traditional story-telling for which Stevenson himself spoke. Romance which relies on predictable elements of suspense and melodrama is likely to reproduce the experience of wonder with the diminishing success of a habit-forming drug. We should look upon wonder as an admirable literary side-effect, rather than as a deliberate aim.

Perhaps the nearest approximation to a genuine literature of the marvellous is to be found in folk-tales and fairy-tales. The earliest critic to stress the parallel between these stories and modern science fiction was Yevgeny Zamyatin, whose 1922 essay on Wells hailed him as a creator of 'urban fairy-tales'. The basis of the modern fairy-tale was not idle fantasy but the realities of science, and, as Zamyatin noted,

> This sounds very paradoxical at first: exact science and fairy-tale, exactitude and fantasy. But it is so, and has to be so. After all, myth is always, whether explicitly or implicitly, connected with religion, and the religion of the present-day city is the exact sciences, so that there is the most natural connection between the latest urban myth, the urban fairy-tale, and science.[8]

It seems ironic that this 'paradox' has recently become an article of faith for a group of contemporary American critics, many of whom, one suspects, are not aware of its source in Zamyatin's brilliant essay. The description of science fiction as a 'contemporary mythology' has received widespread support within the Science Fiction Research Association and the Science Fiction Writers of America.[9] The problem with this idea – and also with Zamyatin's proposition about the 'religion of the present-day city' – is its vagueness. Terms like 'mythology' and 'religion' are being used in a metaphorical way that has almost nothing to do with the functions of the great myths and religions of the past for the societies which produced them. It is true that science fiction offers a collection of stories dealing with the prospects and destiny of man and his civilization. Yet these stories of galactic empires, alien encounters, and the mechanization of human life are deliberate fictions occupying a somewhat marginal place in modern culture. Even where their predictions coincide with those of scientists themselves, their authority is felt in the culture at large to be much less than scriptural. Thus science fiction can only be the 'mythology' of a sub-culture, or, in other words, of fandom. Yet – in another sense of this notoriously slippery term – its mythic status is shared with a very wide variety of social phenomena. Susan Sontag has classified SF films as a form of 'popular mythology',[10] while Roland Barthes has a brief section on Jules Verne in a book (*Mythologies*, 1957) which discusses, *inter alia*, wrestling, striptease, advertising, and photo-journalism. Both Barthes and Sontag see myth as a mode of illusion acting to allay social anxieties and to disguise the realities of power and oppression in the modern world. As Barthes succinctly puts it, myth is 'depoliticized speech'. Thus two quite separate inferences may be drawn from the description of science fiction as 'contemporary mythology'. On the one hand, it gives imaginative expression to the belief-structures of a small group of devotees, and, on the other, it is one of the many vehicles of present-day ideological fantasy.

Functions and formulas

Literary narrative, according to Northrop Frye, is based upon a complication of certain archetypal formulas which may be studied in primitive culture. If science fiction is indeed a species of modern fairy-tale, we might expect its formulaic basis to be unusually explicit. Yet it is clear that the repeated elements that empirical analysis discovers in SF texts fall short of the imperious expectations of the myth-critics and structuralists. The new discipline of structuralist 'narratology' traces its lineage back to the Russian Formalist critics, and especially to Vladimir Propp, whose *Morphology of the Folk-Tale* (1928) is the most concerted attempt in modern criticism to identify the set of formulas common to a given class of narratives. Propp starts from a perception of the twofold quality of folk-tales, which are 'amazingly multiform, picturesque, and colorful', and yet at the same time essentially uniform and recurrent.[11] His explanation of this is that the actions and characters of the stories are governed by a small number of underlying 'functions', comparable to the grammatical functions out of which sentences are constructed. He then goes boldly on to propose the following axioms:

1 Functions serve as stable, constant elements in folk-tales, independent of who performs them, and how they are fulfilled by the dramatis personae. They constitute the components of a folk-tale.
2 The number of functions known in the fairy-tale is limited.
3 The sequence of functions is always identical. . . .
4 All fairy-tales, by their structure, belong to one and the same type.[12]

Propp suggests that the plausibility of his functional analysis of actual folk-tales is a measure of our historical detachment from them, so that in the distant future – but only then – it may become possible to trace the 'phenomena of schematism and repetition' throughout realistic literature.[13] More recent structuralist critics have seized on this cautious statement to sanction their attempts to demystify or deconstruct the particularity of the modern realist text here and now. Without going into the details of Propp's account of the 'functions', however, it may be suggested that his fourth axiom epitomizes the reductiveness of all such methods of analysis. For while he announces that 'all fairy-tales . . . belong to one and the same type' with a scarcely-veiled air of scientific triumph, one may ask what has been done except to give some substance to an existing critical commonplace. We have no difficulty in describing *Oedipus Rex* and *King Lear* as being in certain respects of 'one and the same type'.

Nor, to take examples from the areas of romance and science fiction, is it difficult to see that such diverse texts as *Frankenstein, Dr Jekyll and Mr Hyde*, and *The War of the Worlds* make use of comparable strategies of mystery and suspense and of a set of 'archetypes' such as the Monster, the Double, the Avenger, and the Victim. The recurrence of these archetypes in other contemporary texts, (e.g. *Wuthering Heights*, the novels of Dickens) could, no doubt, be the basis of a theory of nineteenth-century literature and society. Yet, from a literary standpoint, it is the differences between these texts and the individuality of each which continue to fascinate most critics and readers.

It is, of course, rather easy to deflate a structuralist argument by pointing at *King Lear*. Can it be that the very popularity of science fiction and other paraliterary genres constitutes evidence that they are more formulaic and repetitive than the masterpieces of high literature? Such a claim is central to one of the most sustained of recent attempts to analyse popular literary forms, John G. Cawelti's *Adventure, Mystery, and Romance* (1976). Cawelti suggests that the average detective story, western, popular melodrama or SF novel is enjoyed because it is felt to fit into a recognizable narrative pattern and does not pretend to originality. Reading it is a way of entering a 'well-known and controlled landscape of the imagination', in which we recapture the 'security of the familiar': 'the tensions, ambiguities, and frustrations of ordinary experience are painted over by magic pigments of adventure, romance and mystery. The world for a time takes on the shape of our heart's desire.'[14] The model of experience on which this relies is not difficult to describe. 'Ordinary experience' is full of tensions, ambiguities, and frustrations, while literary fantasy provides distraction and solace. It is then quite natural to assume that distraction and solace are the effect of the narrative 'formulas' which Cawelti proceeds to analyse. Yet daydreams and hopeful illusions are rampant in the world of ordinary experience, as well as in literature. Common sense suggests that formulaic writing is as likely to produce

boredom or an ironic tolerance as it is to provide unmiti-
gated pleasure. The aim of reading fiction may well be that
the world for a time should take on 'the shape of our heart's
desire' – but this is true of *all* fiction, or make-believe, and
not just of its more popular varieties. The question is rather
which of the heart's desires a given novel satisfies, and for
how long.

In response to Propp and Cawelti, one has to stress the
sheer inadequacy at present of most generalizations about
formulas and functions in literature. Cawelti's aim is to
avoid the blanket condemnation of popular literature practised by earlier critics, and yet his distinction between popular or 'formulaic' and realistic or 'mimetic' fictional modes is
no less invidious. For not only is it plausible to break down
all narratives into 'functions' in the Proppian manner, but,
more fundamentally still, Cesare Segre has observed that
every form of communication relies on 'schemata', or
'stereotypes of a semiological nature'.[15] The 'expressive
force' of the writer consists in his ability to modify these
schemata and innovate upon their combinations, yet every
fiction which is not identical to an existing fiction must do
this to some extent. We are left with the questions of what is
meant by 'expressive force', why it is manifested in specific
ways in a given genre, and what it is that makes for popularity. Literary theory at present gives little firm guidance in
these areas, and it seems advisable to take a much more
pragmatic and empirical approach to the question of formulas and repeated elements in science fiction.

Domestication

SF is full of repeated elements of one kind and another;
what we must avoid is the temptation to draw over-hasty
conclusions from this. The majority of these elements are
'romantic' in the sense that they involve a certain suspension
of the laws of probability. They have attracted frequent and
often derogatory comment, but nobody has yet catalogued
them systematically. Present-day SF novelists are inclined to

use them knowingly and with ironic intent. We can, indeed, never predict with certainty what their effect will be in a given story.

Characterization in science fiction tends to be formulaic. There have been various explanations for this: the literary incompetence of its authors; the idea that the genre reflects the dehumanization of modern society (Scott Sanders); or that complex characterization detracts from the strangeness of the narrative events (C.S. Lewis).[16] Whichever explanation we choose, there is no doubt of the recurrence of the human stereotypes that Ursula K. Le Guin has labelled 'submyths':

> Superman is a submyth. His father was Nietzsche and his mother was a funnybook, and he is alive and well in the mind of every ten-year-old – and millions of others. Other science-fictional submyths are the blond heroes of sword and sorcery, with their unusual weapons; insane or self-deifying computers; mad scientists; benevolent dictators; detectives who find out who done it; capitalists who buy and sell galaxies; brave starship captains and/or troopers; evil aliens; good aliens; and every pointy-breasted brainless young woman who was ever rescued from monsters, lectured to, patronised, or, in recent years, raped, by one of the aforementioned heroes.[17]

Paraliterary stereotypes, as is evident from this fairly light-hearted list, are often not second- but third-hand, being taken not from life but from earlier varieties of popular fiction. Science fiction's use of such stereotypes is undoubtedly one of the things it has in common with romance rather than with 'high' realism. Yet it also results from the peculiarly dialectical nature of the genre. SF works to 'estrange' the reader by showing him or her a world transformed by some new element. At the same time, this new world is made familiar and thus comprehensible. As Wells wrote, the writer's task is to '*domesticate* the impossible hypothesis'.[18] At the very moment of representing the strangeness of the universe – and the possibilities of change in our own way of existence in the universe – he makes it, in John Huntington's words, 'habitable and . . . basically familiar'.[19] In some SF novels, this leads to a delicately rendered balance between the strange and the familiar; in many others, a superficial exoticism is combined with almost total reassurance that the essentials of life have remained constant. This is the third-rate science fiction that C.S. Lewis condemns in his 'Expostulation':

> Why did you lure us on like this,
> Light-year on light-year, through the abyss,
> Building (as though we cared for size!)
> Empires that cover galaxies,
> If at the journey's end we find
> The same old stuff we left behind,
> Well-worn Tellurian stories of
> Crooks, spies, conspirators, or love,
> Whose setting might as well have been
> The Bronx, Montmartre, or Bethnal Green.[20]

Formulaic characters and plots like these occur *in* science fiction; but they are not characteristic *of* science fiction as opposed to other genres. The process of domestication affects those conventions that make science fiction what it is, as well as the narrative elements that it inherits from other literary forms. This is perhaps inevitable, given the basic purpose of the genre – which is to make scientific or quasi-scientific speculations into the occasion of a satisfying story.

The subgenre of science fiction to which Lewis refers in the lines just quoted is the interstellar space adventure ('space opera'). The conventions that make the space opera possible are, however, of a rather different order from those of 'crooks, spies, conspirators, or love'. The fundamental mode of domestication in the space adventure is that of minimizing the emptiness of space and the chilling remoteness of other star systems. (The chief exception to this rule is the small and distinct group of stories of life aboard multi-generational starships.) If the universe is not shrunken in some convenient way, it is virtually impossible for any human character to take on 'heroic' dimensions. Thus authors whose SF is tinged with romance or heroic fantasy are virtually obliged to make use of faster-than-light travel (FTL), 'space warp' (i.e. the concept of space folding back on itself), or instantaneous 'teleportation' to make the hero's galactic journeys possible. Moreover, there must be 'green worlds', or planets with a biosphere that is not irreducibly hostile to human settlement, in order to give the hero somewhere to go. All this involves an appeal to a beneficent magic in advance of, and perhaps contrary to, contemporary scientific knowledge.

Robert A. Heinlein's *Starman Jones* (1953) is an example of popular science fiction using the 'space warp' convention, and which in many ways fits the definition of a romance. Space-travel in this story is made possible by the existence of 'Horst anomalies' – points at which a highly-skilled team of astronauts can steer their ship through from one side of space to the other. (The concept of folded space can claim some sanction in relativity theory, and it is characteristic of science-fictional conventions in that it is connected both to the actual tendencies of quasi-scientific speculation, such as some of the recent theories about 'black holes', and to further providential plot-developments in the novels in which it occurs.)

Starman Jones is a novel of juvenile heroics concerning the attempts of Max Jones, a young outsider, to become a member of the exclusive professional guild of astronauts. Max has memorized his dead uncle's library of spaceship manuals, and is about to run away from home when the story opens. Since his uncle never fulfilled his promise of nominating him for the astronauts' guild, Max enlists aboard the spaceship *Asgard* under an assumed name. He turns out to be an exemplary crew-member, whose photographic memory and genius for mathematics soon earn him a place in the control room. Later, a navigational error leaves the *Asgard* grounded on a strange planet, with all its technical manuals lost. Thanks to his photographic memory, Max is made acting captain for the homeward voyage.

(There are interesting parallels between his career and that of Luke Skywalker in the film *Star Wars* (1977), though the latter sensationally popular story involves a far more open use of magical fantasy.) As these two examples suggest, conventions like that of 'space warp' are a means of domesticating the science-fictional world by opening it up to the familiar structures of heroic romance. Nevertheless, the texture of *Starman Jones* is predominantly realistic, and one of its most evident models is the nineteenth-century *Bildungsroman*. Max, like David Copperfield, is a provincial young man, done out of his patrimonial inheritance (in his case, a farm in the Midwest), but destined, after a series of trials and errors, to find his niche in the professional middle classes. If his career turns out to be shaped by a poetic justice which, in some respects, might be regarded as virtually magical, the same is true for most of the heroes of nineteenth-century realism. Heinlein's gentle deflation of Max's achievements at the end of the story is also very much in the realistic vein.

Starman Jones is classified by its author as 'juvenile' fiction. Similarly, *Star Wars*, with its adolescent hero and its tinsel princess, would seem to have been deliberately made to extend its appeal to a very young audience. Not surprisingly, these works strike the adult reader as largely formulaic, although, in the case of *Star Wars*, one would have to make allowance for the inventiveness of the technology and costumes, and, in the case of *Starman Jones*, a much greater allowance for the ingenuousness of Heinlein's storytelling and for the intrinsic interest of some of his ideas. Despite Max's inborn prowess and phenomenal good luck, Heinlein presents his actual progress through the ranks of the *Asgard*'s crew as an object-lesson in the rationale of naval discipline, or what he calls the 'politics of the ship'. Thus Max becomes captain because the others are forced to choose him as the only available man qualified to hold this office; and Heinlein holds our attention by his demonstration that this was logically inevitable, even if the outcome strikes us as heavily 'overdetermined'. The 'formulas' invoked are at once romantic and realistic – for example, the *Asgard* is clearly, in one sense, a merchant ship in space, but this enables Heinlein to imagine the working relationships aboard it far more concretely than he could have done otherwise. Thus this relatively simple and 'juvenile' SF work is by no means as easy to categorize as it might appear at first sight. To analyse it into its different levels, archetypal and individual, 'formulaic' and 'mimetic', is one thing; to determine its position in relation to the romantic/realistic Great Divide is quite another. It may, after all, be better to leave Max Jones to his native Ozarks.

Self-conscious romance

What we might call the first-order romance presents an idealized fictional world through its use of traditional storytelling formulas and conventions. It may not succeed in becoming popular, but it has, at least, taken a well-trodden route to its readers' approval. Structuralist analyses of the narrative 'functions' and 'archetypes' reveal the extent to which the apparent diversity of fictional forms may be reduced to repeated elements and patterns. In science fiction, the 'domestication' of the strange and alien phenomena leaves the way open either for realism, or for a fantasy based on recognizable melodramatic patterns, or for something between to two. The divinding-line which separates SF from fantasy (and thus distinguishes, let us say, between *Starman Jones* and *Star Wars*) lies somewhere along this contunuum.

For most practical critical purposes, the terms 'romance' and 'realism' form a convenient pair of opposites. Nevertheless, as Gillian Beer writes, 'At the most general and permanent level it is probably more accurate to see the realistic novel as a mutation of the romance rather than as replacing it'.[21] The dialectical relationship between realism and romance ensures that any fiction whatever contains certain romance elements. These elements may be buried beneath the narrative surface, or, alternatively, they may be on the surface and highlighted. Where the highlighting appears a deliberate part of the artist's method, we may speak of second-order or self-conscious romance. This is the dominant mode in Poe, Stevenson, William Morris, and in the more recent writers of heroic fantasy. The self-conscious romance has (as we saw in chapter 1) played an important part in the development of science fiction. Ursula K. Le Guin's *The Left Hand of Darkness* (1969) is an example of a science-fiction novel with strong romantic elements, which yet remains clearly distinguishable from the productions of modern fantasy.

In Le Guin's 'Hainish' cycle (to which *The Left Hand of Darkness* belongs), the prehistoric inhabitants of Hain have visited a large number of other planets and 'seeded' them experimentally with different kinds of quasi-human stock. The techniques of modern space-travel, developed by the Terrans and Hainish, have led to the progressive rediscovery of these planets, and to their incorporation in the Ekumen or League of Known Worlds. *The Left Hand of Darkness* tells the story of Genly Ai, an envoy sent by the Ekumen to the planet Gethen. The people of Gethen are androgynes who can take on either male or female characteristics during their monthly period of sexual activity; at all other times, their sexuality remains dormant. Gethen also is a very cold world; the Envoy finds it chilly even in the tropics, and the two poles are covered by daunting ice-caps. These points of difference between Gethen and the Earth are the basis of the story, and yet the reader is also aware of some basic similarities. The two principal nations of Gethen, Orgoreyn and Karhide, in some ways resemble Tsarist Russia and imperial China – both vast and, in some areas, very bleak countries. (The names Orgoreyn and Karhide, on the other hand, suggest Le Guin's home state of Oregon and its neighbour Idaho.) One of the main realistic features of the novel is Le Guin's portrayal of the political rivalry between these two semi-feudal states. Furthermore, the fact that Gethen and the other worlds were seeded by the Hainish suggests a universe in which no truly alien intelligence exists. The difficulties of building the Ekumen are thus analogous to – if distinct from – those of bringing together the different nations and cultures on Earth.

Despite his initial mistakes and misunderstandings, Genly Ai succeeds in his mission of persuading Gethen to join the League. His success comes about through the development of a deep personal bond between himself and a disgraced Gethenian statesman, Lord Estraven. Their friendship is cemented as the two fugitives make a daring, three-month-long crossing of the Gobrin ice-cap from Orgoreyn to Karhide. The description of this hazardous journey is a narrative crescendo bringing together most of the novel's themes: the Taoist opposition of dark and light, the ideas of foretelling and mindspeech, the nature of Gethenian sexuality, and, above all, the establishment of unity and trust between two aliens. Meanwhile, the political developments more or less take care of themselves. When the two make their escape from Orgoreyn, their cause seems hopeless; when they arrive back in Karhide – a return for which Estraven pays with his life – it takes very little to persuade the country's king to reverse his earlier decision and join the League. What has happened, as far as the reader is concerned, is that the political change that Genly seeks has been resolved into the drama of change on a personal level, in the coming-together of Genly and Estraven. Such a resolution of social into personal relationships is an inveterate trait of the political novel. Le Guin, however, employs a heavily romanticized version of this: the achievement of union between Genly and Estraven is necessary to the successful conclusion of the novel's great adventure – the journey across the ice.

How do we know that *The Left Hand of Darkness* is second-order rather than first-order romance? The story's affiliations to folk-tales and legends are stressed by the inclusion in the narrative of actual Gethenian folk-tales collected by the Envoy. For example, there is the centuries-old tale of 'Estraven the Traitor' (the present Lord Estraven has committed treachery in the eyes of his king by putting the interests of mankind as a whole before those of Karhide). The opening sentence of Genly's narrative states his somewhat unusual decision to make his official report 'as if I told a story, for I was taught as a child on my homeworld that Truth is a matter of the imagination'.[22] The culmination of this self-reflexive strain comes at the end of the novel, when we see Genly's story itself assuming the status of a legend to be handed down to future generations. Some time after the death of Estraven (he is mown down, on the king's instructions, by Karhidish border-guards) Genly Ai goes on a pilgrimage to his friend's ancestral homeland, the Domain of Estre. The bleak, silent house is presided over by Estraven's father and son – an old man of seventy, and his twenty-year-old heir. The Envoy states his purpose in coming:

'I was with your son in the months before his death. I was with him when he died. I've brought you the journals he kept. And if there's anything I can tell you of those days –'

No particular expression showed on the old man's face. That calmness was not to be altered. But the young one with a sudden movement came out of the shadows into the light between the window and the fire, a bleak uneasy light, and he spoke harshly: 'In Ehrenrang they still call him Estraven the Traitor.'

The old lord looked at the boy, then at me.

'This is Sorve Harth', he said, 'heir of Estre, my sons' son.'

There is no ban on incest there, I knew it well enough. Only the strangeness of it, to me a Terran, and the strangeness of seeing the flash of my friend's spirit in this grim, fierce, provincial boy, made me dumb for a while. When I spoke my voice was unsteady, 'The king will recant. Therem was no traitor. What does it matter what fools call him?'

The old lord nodded slowly, smoothly. 'It matters,' he said.

'You crossed the Gobrin Ice together', Sorve demanded, 'you and he?'

'We did.'

'I should like to hear that tale, my Lord Envoy', said old Esvans, very calm. But the boy, Therem's son, said stammering, 'Will you tell us how he died? – Will you tell us about the other worlds out among the stars – the other kinds of men, the other lives?'[23]

Central to this moving ending are the two demands for stories to be told. The old man wishes to hear the tale of the crossing of the Ice – a heroic narrative in the traditional manner. The boy's hunger, however, is for a full understanding of Estraven's death, and thus for a kind of knowledge reaching beyond his 'homeworld' to 'the other worlds out among the stars'. He will only be satisfied by the full science-fiction narrative that Genly (and, for that matter, Le Guin in her other Hainish novels) has told. Thus *The Left Hand of Darkness*, being at once a romance and a tale of science-fictional realism, satisfies our desire for both the old man's and the young boy's kinds of fictional wonder.

However, there is a price to be paid for this final recognition of the reader's desire – a recognition which, in effect, affirms the fundamental importance of story-telling in any culture which can be called human. For, in this exploration of an androgynous civilization, who can doubt that the sexual roles portrayed in the culminating passage are exclusively male? Despite the references to the 'strangeness' of a kinship system in which one can speak of 'my sons' son', the ending rests on the permanent validity of such archetypes as the father, the son, and the 'fierce provincial boy' (Therem's son 'had a girl's quick delicacy in his looks and movement, but no girl could keep so grim a silence as he did').[24] The artistic dilemma here is a genuine one, for it is almost impossible to evoke the archaic flavour of romance without at the same time reverting to other kinds of cultural conservatism that the writer might wish to avoid. Among our last impressions of Gethen is the realization that it does not seem to be quite as strange a place as might have been expected.[25]

The conclusion that follows from this is that science fiction, for all its romantic components, does not fall naturally into the romance category. In a work like *The Left Hand of Darkness*, a creative tension is set up and, for the most part, maintained between SF and self-conscious romance; but this is a remarkably individual achievement, and not easy to imitate. (Among Le Guin's other works, *City of Illusions* is pure Van Vogtian heroic fantasy, while *The Dispossessed* tends, somewhat awkwardly, towards nineteenth-century realism.)[26] The underlying motive of all romance-writing, as the ending of *The Left Hand of Darkness* suggests so clearly, is that of satisfying our hunger for a pleasing story. SF written as deliberate romance is always likely to end up giving the reader's satisfaction priority over the creation of a rigorously plausible world. Though it belongs as a whole to the category of popular literature, science fiction's most characteristic forms have emerged from its writers' avoidance of the crudest short-cuts to popular success – whether in the forms of the imitation thriller or western, the emotional melodrama, or of what Shelley contemptuously referred to as the 'mere tale of spectres or enchantment'.

4 SCIENCE FICTION AS FABLE

D ESPITE John Keat's opinion that 'We hate poetry that has a palpable design upon us', most science-fiction writers have managed to combine the qualities of the poet and the propagandist. Often they have felt, with H.G. Wells, that art that does not dirty itself with contemporary ideas and opinions is art condemned to triviality. Critics who see science fiction as an essentially didactic genre (as Joanna Russ, for example, has notably done)[1] may be closer to the truth than those who see it as irresponsible popular entertainment.

The traditional 'fable' in the Aesopian sense is a short, simple story with animals as characters, designed to inculcate a moral truth. This is the most rudimentary form of instructive fiction. A less childlike way of sugaring the pill is to be found in the Christian parable, where the agents are not animals but lay figures such as the foolish virgins and the Good Samaritan. Since the agents in any fictional work may be regarded for interpretative purposes as lay figures of this sort, the process of allegory, or, in the broad terms of Angus Fletcher's definition, of 'saying one thing and meaning another'[2] is endemic throughout all literature. No literary text, that is, says all that it signifies. Allegory in the strict sense, however, is confined to works where the communication of a secondary meaning is a deliberate rhetorical intention; it does not apply to those cases where we distinguish between a manifest and a 'latent' content of which the author may be presumed unconscious. In truly didactic fictions, even a surface reading is incomplete unless, at some point, we have become aware of the 'lesson' as separate from the narrative.

Texts which deliberately say one thing and mean another do so for a variety of social reasons. The author may wish to expound and affirm a privileged body of doctrine in a pleasing and memorable way; in this case we have what Suvin calls 'confirmational' allegory,[3] whether in the form of simple didactic stories for children or of the great mythical and religious epics of Dante and Milton. Yet allegory is often used to counter or undermine received doctrines, especially where direct expression would be liable to censorship. The category of subversive or conflictual allegory includes such forms as the parody, the satire, the riddle, and the paradox. The major examples of literary allegory, including the Bible and *Paradise Lost*, include such subversive elements as the relation of the New to the Old Testament, and of Milton's Satan to his God. At the same time, there is a long tradition of 'underground' texts expressing discomforting and heretical views in opposition to the established outlook of literature, philosophy, and theology. Most of the narratives acknowledged as precursors of modern science fiction, whether they are extraordinary voyages, utopias, or *contes philosophiques*, belong in this tradition. Many could only be published posthumously. The marginal literary status which they have usually been accorded is a measure of their negative success in mocking, challenging, or simply going outside existing norms. Lucian, More, Cyrano de Bergerac, Swift, and Voltaire are all masters of subversive allegory.

In the last two hundred years, the various strands of fable and allegory have been profoundly affected by the growth of a liberal, secular reading public, in whom the urge towards rational social understanding is stronger than their commitment to traditional beliefs. Voltaire's *Candide* (1751) shows how the narrative fable was adapted to meet the demands of Enlightenment. Candide himself is, of course, a personification of naivety, but in the space of the story he takes on a more three-dimensional quality than do the lay figures of medieval and Renaissance allegory. Voltaire rounds off the text with an aphorism (*'mais il faut cultiver notre jardin'*) which possesses a richness and irony wholly absent from the maxims at the end of the classical fables.

In terms of imaginative scale and variety, the *conte philosophique* of Voltaire and his contemporaries cannot compare with the 'social novel' as it developed after the French Revolution. In France, Balzac set forth *La Comédie Humaine* as a comprehensive narrative account of the 'comparative anatomy' of human society. In England, Dickens's fictive mission of social enquiry is evident even in an early comic extravaganza such as *The Pickwick Papers*. In his hands the novel became a national institution combining reformists propaganda and journalistic 'exposures' with sentimental entertainment. It was, in effect, part of liberal democracy's self-adjusting and self-transforming mechanism. This change in outlook which the novels of Balzac, Dickens, and their contemporaries embody results from the coming to power of a class dedicated to the 'scientific' ideals of progress and enlightenment, and hence to the abandonment of many of the orthodoxies of the past. As early as 1840, Alexis de Tocqueville was predicting in the second part of his *Democracy in America* that a fiction drawing its imaginative sustenance from the future would soon assume a privileged place in the new bourgeois republics.

Social criticism

In modern literature the terms 'social fable' and 'moral fable' may be applied to almost any fiction in which the author's didactic intentions override his impulses towards artistic (or, for that matter, 'scientific') detachment. Only very rarely – as, for example, in Orwell's *Animal Farm* – is the link maintained with the story about animals. Social fables such as Dickens's *Hard Times* and Elizabeth Gaskell's *North and South* are often joined together with non-fictional writings in a consideration of the literature of protest or 'social criticism'. Admirers of science fiction have always pointed to its role in questioning social assumptions, and today there is widespread recognition of this.[4]

In *New Maps of Hell* (1961), Kingsley Amis describes the genre's 'most important use' as 'a means of dramatising social inquiry, . . . a fictional mode in which cultural tendencies can be isolated and judged'.[5] A number of recent books treat SF as an index to present-day hopes and anxieties about the future.[6]

The idea of science fiction as a mode of social criticism came to the fore in the magazines of the 1950s, when innumerable stories dealt with the threats that new technological developments such as brainwashing, lie-detector tests, computers, and subliminal advertising posed to the freedom of the individual. These stories were a clear response to the militarization of science during and after the Second World War, and to the suppression of dissident views in the McCarthy period – subjects which, as we have seen, were avoided or played down in most other media. Nevertheless, as Robert Bloch argued in Basil Davenport's symposium on *The Science Fiction Novel: Imagination and Social Criticism* (1959), the novelists of the 1950s stopped far short of attacking Western 'free world' ideology at its roots:

> Most social criticism in science fiction novels is not directed against present-day society at all. . . . Our authors, by and large, seem to believe wholly in the profit-incentive; in the trend to superimpose obedience and conformity by means of forcible conditioning; in the enduring liaison between the government, the military and scientists and technologists; in Anglo-Saxon cultural supremacy, if not necessarily outright 'white supremacy'; in the sexual, aesthetic and religious mores of the day. Their criticism of the totalitarian states they envision is merely a matter of degree. . . . When a literature of imaginative speculation steadfastly adheres to the conventional outlook of the community regarding heroes and standards of values, it is indeed offering the most important kind of social criticism – unconscious social criticism.[7]

Even such striking social satires as Kurt Vonnegut's *Player Piano* (1952) and Pohl and Kornbluth's *The Space Merchants* (1953) fail to achieve the sort of radical critique of American values that was to emerge in the 1960s. As late as 1968, a number of the most popular writers, including such redoubtable figures as Robert A. Heinlein and Jack Williamson, sponsored paid advertisements in the *Magazine of Fantasy and Science Fiction* and *Galaxy* in support of the Vietnam war. (The younger, 'New Wave' writers were unanimously in the opposite camp.)[8] While science fiction is indeed a means of 'dramatising social inquiry', in Amis's words, it would be untrue to suggest that its authors have, as a group, pursued such an inquiry more relentlessly or more disinterestedly than their counterparts in realistic fiction.

Cognitive estrangement

While the radicalism of the average SF novel is meagre indeed, it may still be argued that the genre is essentially oriented towards social criticism, just as realistic fiction is oriented towards the study of personal relationships. H.G. Wells wrote that its appeal lay in the 'interest of looking at human feelings and human ways, from the new angle that has been acquired'.[9] The nature of the 'new angle' that science fiction adopts towards empirical reality is the main concern of Darko Suvin's growing body of theoretical writings on the genre. The formal framework of SF, in Suvin's view, is one of 'cognitive estrangement'.[10] It is cognitive by virtue of its affiliation to science and rationality, and estranged by its presentation of a conceptual 'new world' differing from the author's empirical reality. Though any non-realistic narrative might be described as 'estranged' in Suvin's terms, the term carries a strong bias towards social criticism. Ideally, a literature of cognitive estrangement not only facilitates an imaginative 'escape' from or transcendence of the given social environment, but sows the seeds of dissatisfaction with that environment, and of the determination and ability to change it. ('If the world does not please you, *you can change it*', as Wells's Mr Polly discovers.) Science fiction considered as cognitive estrangement offers a series of analogies for, or perhaps imaginative rehearsals of, such possible changes.

The literary concept of estrangement goes back to the Russian Formalist critics of the early twentieth century. In the work of V. Shklovsky and B. Tomashevsky, *ostranenie* ('estrangement' or 'defamiliarization') stands for a cleansing and renewal of our perceptions, brought about by the distancing properties of poetic language. At its simplest level, Shklovsky's use of this idea is strikingly reminiscent of such contemporary aesthetic phenomena as Imagist poetry, and Roger Fry's theory of artistic vision in *Vision and Design* (1920). Unlike the English poets and critics, however, Shklovsky and Tomashevsky extend the concept of estrangement to those narrative forms which force us to see a familiar reality as if for the first time. Their examples include Tolstoy's descriptive method in *War and Peace* and Swift's satirical denunciation of civilization in *Gulliver's Travels*.[11] It should be noted that fictional *ostranenie* is a very broad concept, which could be extended from the most advanced modernist works such as Joyce's *Ulysses* to the simple animal fables with which this chapter began.

Estrangement takes on a more directly social and political significance in the writings of Bertolt Brecht, for whom it functions (in the words of Ernst Bloch) as 'the provision of a shocking and distancing mirror above the all too familiar reality'.[12] This *Verfremdungseffekt* has a potentially transforming effect on the reader or auditor, since it can be used to combat conventional and ideological views of reality by presenting a true picture of man's needs and deprivations. In its scientific aspect, it is exemplified by the great moments of Western discovery, such as Newton's encounter with the falling apple and Galileo's observation of a swinging chandelier: 'He was amazed by the pendulum motion as if he had not expected it and could not understand its occurring, and this enabled him to come at the rules by which it was governed.'[13] The discovery of such 'rules', however, is not only an increase in man's knowledge but an augmentation of his power over his social and natural existence. The phenomenon which has been brought within the realm of rational explanation is revealed, not as natural and inevitable, but as subject to historical intervention and change.[14] Thus the purpose of Brechtian drama is to increase the workers' understanding of possible human relations by piercing bourgeois illusions and revealing the social forces shaping their lives.

If, in Suvin's terms, cognitive estrangement is the 'formal framework' of the science-fiction genre, it must be added that in most cases this framework remains inert. The estrangement-effect of the majority of SF stories is contained and neutralized by their conventionality in other respects. The result is that the familiar reality is replaced by an all too familiar unreality. Thus Suvin's is not so much a descriptive theory of science fiction – a structuralist's pigeonholing device, so to speak – as a highly normative one which asserts that SF has the presentation of a 'distancing' vision, leading to social criticism, as its essential (but usually unfulfilled) promise or purpose.

What is meant by a distancing vision – by a 'shocking and distancing mirror'? Speaking itself in metaphors and from a distance, Suvin's theory says little about the actual processes involved in creating an effect of estrangement. We may imagine a multitude of such effects, ranging from the slight, satirical distortion of reality to the creation of a radical 'otherness' of social structure and experience, based on inspirations from we know not where. Yet even a radical otherness can only be recognized as such by analogy with what is already known. Where we can perceive no grounds for analogy with the familiar, we can perceive no meanings either. The analogy may be negative (a denial of an expected likeness), or positive (an allusion to something unexpected or out of place). Nevertheless, for the reader committed to a view of SF as cognitive estrangement, it can never be wholly gratuitous. For such a reader, a science-fiction tale is always to be understood as a fable is understood. Faced, for example, by Wells's *The First Men in the Moon* with its grotesque civilization of 'flexible-minded messengers', trumpet-faced broadcasters, glass-blowers with enormous lungs and machine-minders with enormous hands, all presided over by a vast braincase like an 'opaque, featureless bladder' – this reader will, like Arnold Bennett, be likely to interpret it as a 'deeply satiric comment on this our earthly epoch of specialisation'.[15] Almost always, he will be right to do so. Yet, it may be asked, what gets left out of such an interpretation, which in effect reduces a work of imagination to its social-critical content?

The work of George Orwell, an avowedly propagandist writer, might be taken to typify the modern fable. *Animal Farm* is a deliberate allegory using animals as characters and then showing, in an amusing twist, that the least pleasant of the animals have become indistinguishable from human beings. *Nineteen Eighty-Four*, after two decades in which it was read with the utmost seriousness as a political prophecy, is now taking its place (along with such predecessors as Jack London's *The Iron Heel*) as a science-fiction story. In this novel Orwell portrays a totalitarian society made possible by new forms of organization, technology, and language, and underpinned by the political theory that the book expounds at length. That is, it is science fiction not because of the future setting but because of the 'estranged' and yet cognitive status of the Thought Police, the two-way telescreen, Newspeak, and Oligarchical Collectivism. At the same time, *Nineteen Eighty-Four* is an intentional, Swiftian distortion of various aspects of contemporary society, ranging from the Nazis to British wartime rationing and the BBC. The novel's opening sentence is: 'It was a bright cold day in April, and the clocks were striking thirteen.' The world introduced by this sentence is not, fundamentally, an unfamiliar one. At most we would tend to react by thinking 'Huh! So they adopted the twenty-four hour clock'. Works in which the author's explicit intention is not one of warning, satire, or exhortations tend to evoke much more ambiguous responses. One may think of the grotesque inventions of

Samuel Butler's *Erewhon*, such as the 'musical banks'. Or of a sentence of Hewinlein's, cited by Samuel R. Delany in a discussion of 'cognitive estrangement': 'The door dilated.'[16] A dilating door is undoubtedly a technological refinement, but we do not immediately perceive why a society would wish to develop it. Or take the following description of an alien creature, from Stanley G. Weinbaum's 'A Martian Odyssey':

> 'The Martian wasn't a bird, really. It wasn't even bird-like, except just at first glance. It had a beak all right, and a few feathery appendages, but the beak wasn't really a beak. It was somewhat flexible; I could see the tip bend slowly from side to side; it was almost like a cross between a beak and a trunk. It had four-toed feet, and four-fingered things – hands, you'd have to call them, and a little roundish body, and a long neck ending in a tiny head – and that beak'.[17]

The beak, it turns out, is not only like an elephant's trunk but like the stem of a plant. The 'bird' can use it to root itself in the ground. This passage begins with a process of definition by negatives (not a bird, not bird-like, not a beak); the paradoxical consequence of this is that almost certainly the reader will start off by visualizing a bird with a beak. Weinbaum's description is fantastic, no doubt, but it is potentially no less science-fictional for that. The voice is that of an amateur naturalist making his first essay in exobiology. In this and the preceding examples, the projection of a strange world involves a certain autonomy, a certain gratuitousness of invention which works against the critic's attempt to reduce the fiction to the status of a fable.

Utopia and scientific materialism

Nineteen Eighty-Four has more often been classified as an anti-utopia than as a science-fiction novel, and the clearest examples of the social fable involving cognitive estrangement are to be found in the utopian tradition. (All utopias also embody a certain amount of gratuitous invention; one need only think of the singular shape of Sir Thomas More's original island.) The study of utopian ideas and narratives now plays a growing role both in literary criticism and in various of the social sciences. The twentieth-century German philosopher Ernst Bloch sees More's conception of a 'no place' which is also a 'good place' as the fundamental locus of the principle of Hope which drives men to try to change society for the better.[18] The question of the relationship between utopia and science fiction is thus of major import. Surveys of utopian and anti-utopian literature, like the studies of social criticism cited earlier, almost invariably include some brief consideration of science fiction. Historians of SF also acknowledge an overlap between the two forms; Rabkin proposes a 'super-genre' consisting of utopia, SF, and satire,[19] while Suvin argues that SF is

> at the same time wider than and at least collaterally descended from utopia; it is, if not a daughter yet a niece of utopia – a niece usually ashamed of the family inheritance but unable to escape her genetic destiny. For all its adventure, romance, popularization, and wondrousness, SF can finally be written only between the utopian and the anti-utopian horizons.[20]

The 'other worlds' of science fiction must always be positively or negatively valued in relation to our own. In the twentieth century, a negative valuation – realized in visions of totalitarian states, a dying Earth, crumbling empires of barbarous and hostile planets – has been the rule. Various commentators have seen this as involving the dire forecast of a 'new dark age'. Others have effusively welcomed those writers whose work shows a reawakening of utopian optimism.[21] Yet, as Suvin implies, the line of descent from utopia to science fiction is not as direct as it might at first seem.

Although science and technology are the principal sources of the material welfare of modern civilization, the idea of a 'scientific utopia' has long seemed to contain a latent, if not an actual, contradiction in terms. Both Fabians and orthodox Marxists have distinguished sharply between the utopian and scientific hopes for social advancement, with the result that 'utopian' was for long a term of abuse on both the communist and the social-democratic left. The earliest portrayal of a scientific utopia in fiction, Bacon's *New Atlantis* (1627), shows a society which lacks the usual utopian attributes of stability, democracy and the abolition of money, and is, therefore, manifestly un-ideal. In nineteenth-century literature there is an open split between the industrialized utopia of Saint-Simon and his successors, of whom the most important was Edward Bellamy in *Looking Backward* (1888), and the pastoral paradises of William Morris's *News from Nowhere* (1890) and W.H. Hudson's *A Crystal Age* (1887). The opposition, as perceived by the late nineteenth century, is between static and dynamic images of the future. The stable societies of Morris and Hudson offer a fulfilment or cessation of human desire, at the price of sociological implausibility (for the reader) and a certain sterility (for the inhabitants). Where, as in *News from Nowhere*, the author allows the survival of some of the sources of restlessness and human conflict, these seem as likely to undermine the happiness that has been achieved as to promote its further improvement. The industrialized utopias, on the other hand, range from euphoric antici-pations of the benefits of advanced capitalism to visions of totalitarian collectivism and the paternalistic manipulation of the individual. To convince the liberal, middle-class reader of the ultimate desirability of such societies is, increasingly, an uphill struggle. (This is the case even in utopias with a strong pastoral element, such as B.F. Skin-ner's *Walden Two*, (1948).) The debunking of utopia exem-plified by Aldous Huxley's *Brave New World* (1932) remains the representative expression of twentieth-century anx-ieties.

In a writer like Huxley, the scorn and cynicism necessary to the satirist are augmented by an attitude of scientific scepticism towards the utopias of earlier generations. Dur-ing the formative period of modern SF, the relationship between 'scientific' and 'utopian' values was widely felt to be one of incompatibility. Utopia was seen as a medium for the subjective longings of the human race; science, for its objective investigations of nature. Scientific positivists appealed (and, in many cases, still appeal) to the ostensible 'facts' of man's genetic endowment, his behavioural needs, and the demands he places upon his environment as witnessing the absurdity of utopian aspirations. SF writers tended to see themselves as spokesmen for this hard-headed attitude, which denies an easy resolution to the inherent problems of man's biological and social 'nature'. Yet science itself is a utopian activity to the extent that it aims to better the lot of mankind. The resulting paradoxes can be traced throughout Wells's work, with its anti-utopian streak running from the portrayal of future degeneration in *The Time Machine* to the bleak denial of all human hopes in *Mind at the End of Its Tether* (1945). In his public pronouncements, Wells was a utopian trying hard to reconcile his faith in continuing human progress with post-Darwinian scientific caution. *A Modern Utopia* (1905) is a compromise book, seeking to contain and resolve the opposition of utopia and science. This is not so much an imaginative fable as a meta-utopia, a diluted, pragmatic attempt to salvage whatever seemed most practicable in the earlier utopian visions.

Wells was not only the founding father of modern SF but one of the major spokesmen for the twentieth-century scientific world-view. In the short term, he looked to the improvement of human life through the spread of technology and social planning. In the long term, however, he and other scientific thinkers were well aware of the limits of necessity which must shadow human development. They saw this development not only in a social-historical perspective, but in that of a natural history which encompassed the formation and death of stars and planets, the slow evolution of living organisms, and the unceasing extinction of species which had failed to adapt to their changing environments. Wells's *Outline of History* (1920) was a monumental attempt to join together the narratives of man's social and his natural history.

The late nineteenth century, then, saw the emergence of a

powerful 'scientific' critique of utopianism; Marx and Engels were among those deeply affected by this. The utopians, however, were unable to mount an effective critique of scientific philosophy, and it is only very recently that such a critique has begun to emerge. From a scientific standpoint, the utopian idea seemed to embody an essentially short-sighted quest for communal happiness. Such an idea was easily caricatured – for example, in the Mediterranean 'pleasure cities' to which Wells's character Hedon retreats with his mistress in the short story 'A Dream of Armageddon' (1903). Hedon turns a deaf ear to the call of duty which would send him back to fulfil his political mission in strife-torn northern Europe. Necessity catches up with him, firstly in the form of world war and then of 'biological' realities as he sees his beloved mistress's body eaten by vultures. Like its successors from *We* to *Nineteen Eighty-Four*, this brief anti-utopian fable is a reminder of the grim political context in which utopianism has struggled for survival in our century. At the same time, it illustrates how easily the conflict between utopian and scientific attitudes could be translated into one between individual pleasure and self-sacrificing devotion to duty. In Darwinian terms, the subjective happiness of the individual has no relevance whatever to the prospects and destiny of the species; the 'end of life' in the animal kingdom is to reproduce successfully and to protect one's young. ('Survival' for the individual, that is, simply means survival to the age of reproduction.) While Darwin's theory does not in itself provide a sufficient basis for moral behaviour, 'evolutionary ethics' attempts to find a common ground between the 'truths' of biology and the traditional criteria of civilized morality. Wells's own conclusion was that the search for private and personal fulfilment is illusory, since man's true source of identity is his membership of a growing and ever-experimenting species.

The modern scientific world-view derives not only from biology but from physics, astronomy, biology, and (more recently) cybernetics. One of its main tenets is the smallness of man in the impersonal space-time universe of present-day cosmology. Yet man, for all his insignificance, has knowledge of the cosmos, and it is a basic principle of the scientific attitude that knowledge can be turned into power. The more we know of the forces of 'nature', the more likely it is that we can control them. SF stories considered as fables may roughly be divided into two classes: epistemological fables or fables of knowledge, such as *The Time Machine* and Stanislaw Lem's *Solaris*, and fables of power such as Blish's *A Case of Conscience*, Clarke's *Childhood's End*, and most of the tales of the Strugatsky brothers. The two categories, admittedly, overlap a good deal; but it is in their capacity as fables of power that science-fiction tales tend to become specifically anti-utopian. In Milton's *Paradise Lost*, Satan tempts Eve with the promise that eating of the Tree of Knowledge will confer a godlike power on her and her progeny. Utopia, like Eden, is normally a place without political conflict. Modern science's aim of mastery over nature is not only radically unsettling in its social effects, it is also an inherently political aim. As C.S. Lewis wrote, 'we are always conquering Nature, *because* "Nature" is the name for what we have, to some extent, conquered.' And further: 'The power of Man to make himself what he pleases means . . . the power of some men to make other men what *they* please.'[22]

The utopian social ideal is normally one of face-to-face community. Wells and his intellectual successors turned away from this ideal to that of the 'mind of the race' confronting the unknown. The contemporary representatives of the 'mind of the race' are the privileged élite of the scientifically-minded who have emancipated themselves from traditional loyalties. The scientists form an 'avant-garde', pioneering the way that civilization as a whole must follow if it is to avoid self-destruction. This avant-gardist philosophy of science found classic expression in J.B.S. Haldane's essay *Daedalus: or, Science and the Future* (1923). 'If every physical and chemical invention is a blasphemy, every biological invention is a perversion,' Haldane wrote. 'The scientific worker of the future will more and more resemble the lonely figure of Daedalus as he becomes conscious of his ghastly mission, and proud of it.'[23] The conviction that the efforts of the 'scientific worker', however ghastly they might be, were the *sine qua non* of human progress was fundamental to the scientific socialism that Haldane and his colleagues such as J.D. Bernal were to preach in the world communist movement in the 1940s and 1950s.[24] The science fiction of the same period is full of the assumption that, in the future, effective power will or should be in the hands of a scientific élite.

Galactic imperialism

The ultimate symbol of the 'conquest of nature' advocated by modern scientific thinkers is the foundation of a galactic empire. Once he has developed space-travel, man can visibly establish his significance in the universe, and perhaps even aspire to dominate it. The idea that human destiny lies in taking the route to the stars is the most powerful alternative to the traditional utopian visions that science fiction has to offer. In pulp SF, the galactic empire may be controlled by humanity and menaced by alien or dissident elements, or it may be an instrument of alien oppression threatening the Earth. In either case, it is invariably a theatre of war. Such stories are at once a projection of twentieth-century imperialist violence and a *prediction* of a non-utopian future in which the brute facts of power and self-assertion will remain very much what they are. Considered as territory ripe for colonization, the universe may appear as a virgin land empty save for a few shiftless natives, as an ocean in which little green men are constantly threatening the trade-routes, or even as a complex division of superpowers and spheres of interest. Man may no sooner have left the Earth than he discovers super-civilized aliens whose mission is to bring fire and the sword or, alternatively, the extraterrestrial equivalents of Bibles and beads, to benighted humanity. All these are variants on the basic model of the imperialist vision. The galactic empires of the pulps are echoed at a higher level by the 'expansionist' convictions of such writers as Wells, Stapledon, and Heinlein. The opposition between utopian 'complacency' and scientific empire-building, for example, is stated very plainly at the climax of the Wells–Alexander Korda film *Things to Come* (1935):

> PASSWORTHY: My God! Is there never to be an age of happiness? Is there never to be rest?
>
> CABAL: Rest enough for the individual man. Too much of it and too soon, and we call it death. But for MAN no rest and no ending. He must go on – conquest beyond conquest. This little planet and its winds and ways, and all the laws of mind and matter that restrain him. Then the planets about him, and at last out across immensity to the stars. And when he has conquered all the deeps of space and all the mysteries of time – still he will be beginning.[25]

Cabal here is a spokesman for the doctrine that C.S. Lewis was to attack in *The Abolition of Man* (1943) and in his SF novels of the same period as 'human racism'. Passworthy's opinions are those of the reactionary populist movement, led by the sculptor Theotocopulos, which at the close of *Things to Come* seems on the verge of overwhelming Cabal and his followers. But – since scientific imperialism always takes the 'long-term view – we may be confident that such a defeat for scientific values is only temporary. What Wells and many other science-fiction writers point to is an eventual 'parting of the ways' leading to a bifurcation of the human race, either as the survivors and the extinguished or as those who are leaving and those who choose to remain on the planet Earth. J.D. Bernal, in his remarkable book of scientific anticipations, *The World, The Flesh and the Devil* (1929), envisaged such a 'dimorphism' of humanity, adding that those who stayed on Earth might end up as a 'human zoo' – 'a zoo so intelligently managed that its inhabitants are not aware that they are there merely for the purposes of observation and experiment'.[26]

Things to Come, like nearly all of Wells's SF, early and late, may be regarded as a fable of power. Wells's earlier and best-known fables are all deeply ambiguous; as Suvin writes, 'he is a virtuoso in having it ideologically both ways'.[27] In *The War of the Worlds*, for example, the imperialism of the Martians meets its Nemesis at the hands of the terrestrial bacteria against which, as aliens, they have no immunity. Yet this is by no means a single-mindedly anti-imperialist tale, since the Martians' path of escape from their native planet is one which mankind must eventually follow. Wells's Epilogue hints strongly that the two races are destined to compete for the mastery of the universe:

> We have learned now that we cannot regard this planet as being fenced in and a secure abiding-place for Man; we can never anticipate the unseen good or evil that may come upon us suddenly out of space. It may be that in the larger design of the universe this invasion from Mars is not without its ultimate benefit for men; it has robbed us of that serene confidence in the future which is the most fruitful source of decadence, the gifts to human science it has brought are enormous, and it has done much to promote the conception of the commonweal of mankind. . . . It may be, on the other hand, that the destruction of of the Martians is only a reprieve. To them, and not to us, perhaps, is the future ordained.[28]

The ultimate benefit that the invasion may have brought is scarcely utopian. Even the 'conception of the commonweal of mankind' seems intended, in this context, only to turn the human race into a more efficient military unit.

Liberation and power

Hard-headed galactic imperialism would not be as prevalent as it is in SF if its premises were wholly without intellectual justification. The reproach that it brings against classical utopianism – even in the crude terms in which Wells's Cabal expressed it to Passworthy – is a valid one. Man has little hope of achieving a civilization in which he can one day 'knock off', with his conflicts resolved and his restlessness stilled. Rather, in the famous lines of Andrew Marvell (though the context, a defence of Cromwell's subjugation of the Irish, is scarcely a propitious one), 'The same *Arts* that did *gain*/A *Pow'r* must it *maintain*.' To juxtapose these lines with the contemporary socialist view that utopia means 'a way of life qualitatively different *in every respect* from that of capitalism'[29] is to appreciate the dilemma of the modern utopianist. Since the late 1960s there has been a dramatic revival of interest in utopian ideas in the West. At the same time, the ideals of mastery over nature and of the perfection of the social organization have given way, to a large extent, to that of liberation from oppression. The libertarian ideal is, of course, as problematic as any other political principle. In the first place, it presupposes that there is within humanity an infinite but frustrated potential for successful experimentation and self-realization. Once this is granted, the liberationist is committed to the faith that self-realization is necessarily benign rather than destructive in its social effects. In its predictive aspects, the result is a perspective of ongoing (and perhaps never-ending) dialectical struggle against new forms of 'oppression' – a vision in sharp contrast both with the static perfection of the traditional utopias and the hypostatization of man's ultimate destiny in post-Darwinian science.

The changing outlook of contemporary utopianism is paralleled to some extent by new developments in the philosophy of science. Scientific 'truths' – above all, in their reliance on general concepts such as those of man, space, time, and nature – are now seen to be inherently anthropomorphic and subject to revision. The supposed objectivity of laws and theories has been challenged by the realization that they invariably reflect, at some level, the structures of thought and social relationships in the societies which produce them. In the case of a popular-scientific concern such as space-travel, this statement is almost a truism. Nobody could doubt that the actual US/USSR space-race was a form of sublimated imperialism. It might now seem that the 'conquest' of nearby planets, whether by

indomitable space-captains and their flagships or by
unmanned scientific probes, is one thing; their understanding is quite another. A contemporary physicist sums up the
new cosmology by saying that 'the more the universe seems
comprehensible, the more it also seems pointless'.[30] In this
situation (as various SF writers have indicated), the best we
could do might be to attempt to understand ourselves, and
our own thirst for such evanescent knowledge.

In the most recent science fiction, the fables of power
have become tentative and ambiguous, and often – as, for
example, in such a popular success as Frederik Pohl's *Gate-
way* (1977) – have turned into fables of impotence. The hero
struggling, like Joe Fernwright in Philip K. Dick's *Galactic
Pot-Healer* (1971), to hold together some fragments in a
disintegrating universe is now a commonplace figure.
Galactic imperialism is taken for granted, perhaps in
response to the actual achievement of space-flight; it is the
disturbing consequences of this attempt at territorial expansion that must now be faced. The empire-building ideal
itself survives, in a liberal rather than libertarian version, in
Le Guin's Hainish novels discussed in the previous chapter.
According to Genly Ai in *The Left Hand of Darkness*, membership of the Ekumen or League of Known Worlds is entirely
voluntary, and yet is something a world will naturally choose
once it has emerged out of the 'dark ages' to reach a certain
level of social development.[31] The Ekumen, however, is a
utopian community because its doctrine is 'just the reverse
of the doctrine that the end justifies the means'.[32] Genly's
exposition of the politics of the Ekumen involves a re-
adjustment, rather than a wholly satisfactory alternative, to
the ideals of galactic imperialism;

> . . . the Ekumen is not essentially a government at all. It is
> an attempt to reunify the mystical with the political, and
> as such is of course mostly a failure; but its failure has
> done more good for humanity so far than the successes of
> its predecessors. It is a society and it has, at least poten-
> tially, a culture. It is a form of education; in one aspect it's

a sort of very large school – very large indeed. The motives of communication and co-operation are of its essence, and therefore in another aspect it's a league or union of worlds, possessing some degree of centralized conventional organization. . . . The Ekumen as a political entity functions through co-ordination, not by rule. It does not enforce laws; decisions are reached by council and consent, not by consensus or command. As an economic entity it is immensely active, looking after interworld communications, keeping the balance of trade among the Eighty Worlds. . . . Now if the Ekumen, as an experiment in the superorganic, does eventually fail, it will have to become a peace-keeping force, develop a police, and so on.[33]

The Left Hand of Darkness, in this aspect, is a political fable, speaking with the slightly tedious explicitness of the utopia, and – as Sir Thomas More said that he spoke – of 'things . . . that I wish rather than expect to see followed among our citizens'. SF in the twentieth century has, in its more sombre moments, stressed the expectations rather than the wishes of the age; at other times, it has made visionary projections out of the will to power of a scientific avant-garde. It is too early to detect any widespread change in this pattern, though it seems likely that the conflict between science and utopia will continue to reproduce itself in new forms as the genre develops. Whatever their other literary characteristics, a large proportion of SF novels have something to say about the issues of knowledge and power. They tend to demand with a peculiar insistence to be read, in part, as social parables or fables.

5 SCIENCE FICTION AS EPIC

From Verne and Wells to the novelists of the 1940s and 1950s who anticipated the developments of space-flight, a significant proportion of SF writers have been listened to not only as social critics but as social prophets. Today newspapers, magazines, radio, and television supply an eager audience for the visions of tomorrow painted by novelists and scientific popularizers such as Isaac Asimov and Arthur C. Clarke. Science fiction is viewed in some quarters as a branch of futurology, or the science of social forecasting. According to Heinlein's definition discussed in chapter 1, the method of SF is in any case one of 'extrapolation' from the present to the future. The 'tale of the future' or future history has its own scholars and bibliographers, and is often assumed by outsiders to be coextensive with science fiction as a whole.

The act of becoming a 'prophet' entails the deliberate projection of speculative hypotheses, whether or not these are cast in the form of fiction. Our society combines scepticism about the possibilities of foretelling with a great hunger for intimations of what the future will hold. Those who attempt to satisfy this hunger are engaging in prophecy, yet even the most visionary of modern thinkers are 'prophets' only by metaphorical courtesy. The great majority of visions of the future, that is – including many of those belonging to scientific futurology – have no genuinely cognitive status except as reflections on the forces operative in the present in which they are made. Suvin writes that 'the cognitive value of all SF, including anticipation-tales, is to be found in its analogical reference to the author's present rather than in predictions, discrete or global'.[1] Narratives of future history are a form of make-believe – a property which they share with all other fiction. In fact, it is only when considerations of predictive accuracy are put to one side that we can begin to understand the future history's powerful appeal to the modern imagination. The tale of the future is the main representative of the epic mode in science fiction – epic being defined in modern terms by Ezra Pound as a 'poem including history'.[2]

The inclusion of history marks the contrast between the epic and the romance. Epic writing lacks the arbitrariness that Gillian Beer attributes to the romance, and its purpose is never simply to hold its audience spellbound. The dignity and seriousness of the classical *epos* reflects the fact that the heroic deeds it recounts are supposed to have really taken place, while the secondary epics of Dante and Milton lay claim to a profound religious and symbolic truth. Where the romance may be written in a whimsical and parodic manner, drawing attention to the imaginary nature of the world it depicts, epic writing postulates a historical or eschatological continuity between the events it narrates and the reader's situation. These events have both a specified time and place in the 'historical world', and a permanent national or religious significance for the social group to whom the epic belongs. And while the intervention of gods and goddesses in human affairs is a regular feature of traditional epic, this is portrayed in terms of recognizably human motivations of pity, affection, benevolence, jealousy, and spitefulness, rather than as part of an undifferentiated supernatural. The epic is thus a secular or historical narrative of events and deeds which constitute the heritage, or provide the key to the destiny, of the people for whom it is written.

A debased use of the term 'epic' is one of the most regular features of the promotional material on SF put out by publishers and film companies. It may, indeed, be the mindless reiteration of the term on paperback covers and movie posters which has led to its comparative neglect by critics of the genre. 'Epic' science fiction in the commercial sense invariably involves space-travel, since space is the last natural frontier, and thus the appropriate setting for a new heroic age of exploration, adventure, and imaginary wars. The story of how the Earth, or some other homeland, was saved is a plausible substitute for the old national epic, concerned with the establishment and defence of the realm. Nevertheless, the run-of-the-mill 'space epic' is usually decked out with the stock figures and situations of conventional romance: villainous monsters, enchanted landscapes, plucky young heroes and princesses born to send brave men to their deaths. The new heroic age of exploration repeats the discovery of America (we may even end up on a beach with the ruins of the Statue of Liberty, as in the film of Pierre Boulle's *Planet of the Apes*), while the story of how the Earth was saved turns into a comic game of cops and robbers or a re-run of the Second World War. The presence of detailed technical descriptions may help to give the impression of verisimilitude, and thus of a genuine approximation to epic form. The 'hard' technology of *2001: A Space Odyssey* might be compared to Homer's itemization of military equipment, while the purely decorative spacecraft of *Star Wars* are reminiscent of the horses and armour of chivalric romance. However, the principal grounds for calling some science fiction epic as opposed to romantic are that it deals with future or alternative history. The plausibility that such stories share with realism is as essential as the heroic deeds and fateful contests that they share with modern fantasy.

SF and the historical novel

The events portrayed in epic fiction must be of a certain magnitude. Though they need not be noble deeds in the old sense, they must involve the fate not of individuals but of whole societies, or of the human race, its collaterals or descendants. Science fiction is often closer than realistic fiction to the old epics, by virtue of its universal scale, the scope it allows for heroic enterprise, and its concern with

man's confrontation with non-empirical and extraterrestrial forces. Nevertheless, SF which takes the form of a
'fictive history'[3] has often been likened to realism. H.G.
Wells suggested that the 'futurist story . . . should produce
the effect of an historical novel the other way round'.[4] He
was referring to the 'illusion of reality' that it ought to
sustain. Though both are related to traditional epic, the idea
that the future history and the historical novel are mirror-
images of one another is to some extent a chronological
illusion. Bad historical novels and bad science fiction tend to
resemble one another, since both rely on the stereotypes of
the romance genres; the essential difference, however, between the fictional bringing-to-life of a past world and the
invention of a future one is that between historiography and
speculation or anticipation.

The great Marxist critic Georg Lukács follows Hegel in
arguing that all the modes of modern realism are descendants of the ancient epic. The progressive alienation of man
from his fellow-men since the dawn of Greek civilization
accounts, in his view, for the passing away of the primitive
epic form with its direct expression of the 'extensive totality
of life'. The bourgeois novel attempts to recapture the unity
of Homer's 'rounded universe' through its portrayal of the
social trajectory of the 'problematic hero'.[5] In *The Historical
Novel* (1936-7) Lukács argues that the novelists whom he
calls 'critical realists' are able to evoke the totality of the
process of social development by means of their portrayal of
conflict between 'typical individuals'. (The concept of
characters as representative 'types', it should be noted, is a
modern innovation which implies a combination of the epic
form with allegory or fable.) The pioneer of the modern
realist epic, in Lukács' view, is Sir Walter Scott.

Lukács' key distinction in *The Historical Novel* between the
'classical form' of Scott's historical novels and the naturalistic costume-drama exemplified by Flaubert's *Salammbô* is
helpful in considering the nature of science fiction's historical narratives. Scott's novels, according to Lukács, have as
their underlying theme the social transformations which

have led to the emergence of modern Britain. He shows these historical crises as they were experienced within the 'being of the age' – the broad sweep of everyday life. The conflicts undergone by Scott's 'middle-of-the-road' heroes are those which, in retrospect, may be seen as constituting a decisive parting of the ways in national development. These conflicts are portrayed with a degree of 'necessary anachronism', since Scott allows his characters to express 'feelings and thoughts about real, historical relationships in a much clearer way than the actual men and women of the time could have done'.[6] In this way the period in which the novel is set is revealed as part of an essential history leading up to the present.

Flaubert in *Salammbô* portrays a society (that of ancient Carthage in conflict with the Barbarians) which has no direct historical connection with his own. His novel expresses a 'scientific' attitude in its reliance upon historical and archaeological research and its elimination of any sort of anachronistic historical awareness on the part of its characters. The attractions of *Salammbô* for the reader lie simply in its exoticism and in what Lukács calls its 'pseudo-monumentality'. However, the exoticism is only superficial, since the emotional conflicts of the protagonists are characterized by an implicit 'modernization':

> Artists have admired the accomplishment of Flaubert's descriptions. But the effect of Salammbô herself was to provide a heightened image, a decorative symbol, of the hysterical longings and torments of middle-class girls in large cities. History simply provided a decorative, monumental setting for this hysteria, which in the present spends itself in petty and ugly scenes, and which thus acquired a tragic aura quite out of keeping with its real character.[7]

The mode that Lukács is describing here is that of the historical costume-drama, in which characters in alien settings and exotic dress are shown pursuing desires of a basically familiar and conventional kind. The pseudo-monumentality that Lukács detects is all too familiar in 'historical' science fiction, whether the futures it depicts are embodiments of glittering rationality or of neo-feudal brutality and splendour. Indeed, the great majority of really lengthy SF novels and 'epics' are costume-dramas of considerable banality.

Truncated epic

Is there, however, a 'classical' form of epic science fiction comparable to that which Lukács discovered in the historical novel? Since there are no credible equivalents to the Waverley novels or *War and Peace*, it has sometimes been suggested that the 'great epic' of science fiction has yet to be written.[8] Yet it must be remembered that future histories differ profoundly from the historical novels of the nineteenth century in that their basis is not history but speculation or prophecy.

The science fiction that may be called 'prophetic' invokes the authority of the modern cognitive sciences for its speculations about the far future. (We are not concerned here with Jules Verne-like speculations about the very *near* future, in which the vast majority of social data remain unchanged.) The major problem of this mode of writing – one identified by Wells in his remarks about the 'futurist' story – is that while the future history may be convincing in outline, it is very difficult to keep it convincing in detail. The greater the wealth of fictional incident, the greater the reader's awareness is likely to be that he is faced not with logical necessity but with hypothetical, and often gratuitous, fantasy. For this reason, science-fiction writers have good reason for sheering away from traditional epic construction in their narratives of the future. The characteristic relationship of many SF stories to the older epics is, it would seem, one of truncation or frustration. If the events that they portray are of epic magnitude, the manner of their portrayal is brief and allegorical, reminiscent not of the poem in twelve books but of the fables discussed in the previous chapter.

A major example of the truncated epic (or 'epic fable') in science fiction is Wells's *The Time Machine*, the story of a voyage of thirty million years into the future which is told in little over 30,000 words. The (unnamed) Time Traveller, a representative nineteenth-century scientist and inventor, comes, as he tells us, 'out of this age of ours, this ripe prime of the human race, when Fear does not paralyse and mystery has lost its terrors'.[9] He embarks on a Promethean mission, since, from the viewpoint of post-Darwinian evolutionism, knowledge of the future could transform man's sense of the meaning and possibilities of his existence. Wells does not disappoint us of his promise to give a comprehensive and prophetic account of the future. It might be objected that his brevity in doing so was determined by the publishing conditions of the 1890s, but in fact Wells was exploiting a newly-won freedom to publish short fiction, rather than being forced to confine himself to a certain length. The prospect of *The Time Machine* in three volumes did not appeal to its author, and does not appeal to the reader.[10]

The reason for this lies not only in Wells's didactic intentions, but in the nature of the scientific thought on which the story is based. The plausibility of *The Time Machine*'s prophecy of the future is proportional, in large part, to the abstract and inhuman nature of the laws of evolution, thermodynamics, and class struggle invoked by the Time Traveller to explain what he sees. Wells could have invented more episodes to show the various intermediate stages of the future, and especially the epoch of man's supremacy – a period which he passes over in virtual silence. In fact, as he revised the story, he actually suppressed at least one episode. The story as it stands has an air of historical inevitability, from which further fanciful invention could only detract.

There are two major prophecies in *The Time Machine*: that of the degeneration of human civilization as represented by the Eloi and the Morlocks, and that of the gradual regression of all life on Earth to the point reached in the final scenes on the beach. The episode of the Eloi and Morlocks, although a demonstration of evolutionary decline, seems to embody a warning of the possible consequences of the greed, complacency, and rigid class divisions of present society. Wells here is satirizing both the society in which he grew up (the 'overground' and 'underground' races paralleling the rigid stratification of the country house in which his mother was housekeeper), and the peacefully prosperous societies which utopians such as William Morris foresaw in the near future. The effect is to make sense of man's possible future, since this future appears as the outcome of social choices made in the present. It may be questioned whether the same logic applies to the final scenes, where the progressive extinction of all higher forms of life as a result of planetary cooling is an unforgettable expression of cosmic pessimism. In theory it is possible for mankind to avoid the fate reserved for life on Earth – by migrating into space – but this possibility is not mentioned in the story. Rather, the vision of implacable biological Necessity confronting man fulfils the prophetic intimations that came upon the Time Traveller as he gazed, fascinated, upon the 'winged sphinx' at the moment of his entry into the world of 802,701:

> A colossal figure, carved apparently in some white stone, loomed indistinctly beyond the rhododendrons through the hazy downpour. But all else in the world was invisible. . . . It chanced that the face was towards me; the sightless eyes seemed to watch me; there was the faint shadow of a smile on its lips. It was greatly weather-worn, and that imparted an unpleasant suggestion of disease. *I stood looking at it for a little space – half a minute, perhaps, or half an hour*. It seemed to advance and to recede as the hail drove before it denser and thinner. At last I tore my eyes from it for a moment, and saw that the hail curtain had worn threadbare, and that the sky was lightening with the promise of the sun.
>
> *I looked up again at the crouching white shape, and the full temerity of my voyage came suddenly upon me*. What might

appear when that hazy curtain was altogether with-drawn? What might not have happened to men? What if cruelty had grown into a common passion? What if in this interval the race had lost its manliness, and had developed into something inhuman, unsympathetic, and overwhelmingly powerful? I might seem some old-world savage animal, only the more dreadful and disgusting for our common likeness – a foul creature to be incontinently slain.[11] (My emphases.)

It is only after this trance-like examination of the sphinx that the Time Traveller is able to make out any other details of the future world. (It is notable that Wells does not describe him taking his eyes off the sphinx the second time; rather, the whole landscape becomes visible behind and around the sphinx.) The statue of the sphinx is an embodiment of the awesomeness of the prophetic vision, which the Time Traveller himself experiences as 'the full temerity of my voyage'. His fear of finding himself in the grip of over-whelming power is not realized in the world of 802,701 (in which he appears almost godlike to the Eloi, and is able to meet the Morlocks on more or less equal terms), but in the 'Further Vision' where he confronts, not the descendants of humanity, but the 'inhuman, unsympathetic, and over-whelmingly powerful' force of entropy which is bringing about the death of the solar system. The epic quality of the story results not only from its projection of future history but from the Time Traveller's courage in facing the evi-dence of mankind's futility and bringing it back to his hearers. He is committed to observing what lies in store for humanity (although he can do no more than observe it), however appalling that knowledge may be. His personal heroism is finally proved by his readiness to embark on a second journey into time – the one from which he never returns. The ambivalence with which a more ordinary humanity must regard such heroism and such prophecy is implied by the narrator's remarks in the Epilogue:

He, I know – for the question had been discussed among

us long before the Time Machine was made – thought but cheerlessly of the Advancement of Mankind, and saw in the growing pile of civilisation only a foolish heaping that must inevitably fall back upon and destroy its makers in the end. If that is so, it remains for us to live as though it were not so. But to me the future is still black and blank – is a vast ignorance, lit at a few casual places by the memory of his story.

The final phrase is a reminder of the difference between prophecy and historiography, and also of the tentativeness that afflicts all modern epic writing (whether or not it is science-fictional), since there is always a level at which the hero's deeds seem gratuitously inflated and the narrative is 'only a story'. The fact is that no artist's vision today can mould his society as inescapably as Homer did his.

The Time Machine, then, is a narrative of heroism and prophecy in which the degree of dramatization exactly corresponds to the authority of the 'laws of future history' which it invokes. While it is the element of dramatization which constitutes the difference between science-fictional prophecies and those of 'futurology',[12] it remains true that *The Time Machine* would not exist were it not for the anticipative and eschatological tendencies inherent in the scientific thought of Wells's time. The process of extrapolation from the present into the future reflects the basic promise of science, which is that all things can in principle be known because they are subject to 'natural law'. Yet it has already been argued that 'anticipations' belong in the category of fictions and hypotheses, rather than to scientific knowledge. Logically they do not differ from models of the world based on premises admitted to be fantastic, provided that the latter models are self-consistent. The most that can be said of them is (in Isaac Asimov's words) that 'sometimes such extrapolations are fairly close to what happens'.[13] In addition, our response to them is often a factor in determining whether or not they are close to what happens.

Scientific anticipation

Apart from simple assumptions of the order of 'If this goes on . . .,' twentieth-century science fiction has two basic rational methods of projecting the future – those of technological determinism and evolutionism. Technological determinism is the belief that man's future will be transformed by technological innovations whose impact it is possible to predict. Evolutionism is the belief that all life is subject to irreversible change under the operation of natural laws such as the need to adapt to its environment or perish. Predictions based on these two beliefs claim the impersonal authority which comes from viewing the future as a process of natural, rather than man-made history. Such authority, however tentative its actual foundations, has had an almost irresistible attraction for certain science-fiction writers.

The basis of technological forecasting is that man's life will be materially transformed in the future as radically, if not far more radically, that it has been in the past. Evolutionism, however, suggests what must be irreparably lost in this process; whether or not mankind is destined to die out like the great dinosaurs, such prophecies invariably involve fundamental changes in human ecology. These prospects have been explored in a growing literature of scientific anticipation, which received great impetus in the earlier twentieth century both from the work of Wells (in fiction and non-fiction) and from the popular writings of scientists such as J.B.S. Haldane and J.D. Bernal. Haldane's *Daedalus: Or, Science and the Future* (1923) and Bernal's *The World, the Flesh and the Devil* (1929) are two seminal works in this tradition. In the present context, Haldane's fictional essay 'The Last Judgment' (1927) will serve as a classic example of pure prophecy involving both technological determinism and evolutionism. 'The Last Judgment' is an eschatological speculation on 'the most probable end of our planet as it might appear to spectators on another'.[14] Haldane begins by discussing possible causes of the eventual catastrophe – the sun might become a supernova, a huge meteor might collide with the Earth, or planetary cooling might take place – but he concludes that a man-made disaster is far more likely. The disaster he envisions is an unforeseen, long-term consequence of man's greatest technological triumph – the harnessing of tidal power as an energy source – which brings about prosperity and happiness on Earth. But, as his future historian writes in what now seems a manifestation of high optimism, 'it was characteristic of the dwellers on earth that they never looked more than a million years ahead, and the amount of energy available was ridiculously squandered'.[15] The eventual result is that the speed of the Earth's rotation begins to diminish, causing unprecedented climatic severity and the extinction of virtually all non-human species. Alarmed by these events, a group of humans band together and set off to colonize Venus. Disease, crime, and unhappiness reappear among them, but they also evolve new senses, one of which is a form of telepathy. Their biological development is so fast that the crew of the last projectile to reach Venus are discovered to be incapable of fertile unions with the existing colonists; as a result (and this is typical of the ruthlessness of the new Venusian breed) the latecomers are 'used for experimental purposes'. Meanwhile, the Earth's moon splits up, and the some of its fragments strike the mother planet, destroying the remnants of terrestrial humanity. The Venusians prepare to recolonize Earth, as well as the remainder of the planets of the solar system, breeding specially equipped races to accomplish each task. Their eventual goal is the conquest of the whole galaxy, and then – since the galaxy may not survive for more than 80 million million years – of the furthest limits of the universe. The death of the Earth is a negligible event in this process.

The substance of Haldane's prophecy is that man faces a choice between emigration to other worlds and extinction on Earth. The prospect of galactic imperialism which he introduces at the end of 'The Last Judgment' – and which is also present in Bernal and the later Wells – was simultaneously providing an 'epic' subject-matter for the contributors to Gernsback's and other SF magazines. Today's reader may well be tempted to moralize about the trail of destruction and sheer wastage of natural and human resources that a race spreading throughout the universe and dedicated to overcoming every challenge of the environment seems likely to leave behind it. Yet, in literary terms, one might as well lament the despoliation in the *Iliad*. In the decades before the achievement of space-flight, galactic imperialism was both a credible prophecy of man's destiny and an ideal framework for the narratives of heroic conflict and resolution which are the legacy of traditional epic. The result was the proliferation of science-fictional costume-drama ('space opera'), and the attempts by writers such as Olaf Stapledon, Arthur C. Clarke, Isaac Asimov, Robert A. Heinlein, and Walter M. Miller, Jr, to create a more serious mode of future history.

The future histories

Stapledon was not a professional novelist in the usual sense, and *Last and First Men* (1930), through all its inordinate length, follows the method of factual historiography. At the same time, it pioneers the projection of a cyclical history, which has become commonplace in more recent science fiction. In *Last and First Men*, humanity and its descendants rise and fall no fewer than thirteen times. As Robert H. Canary points out in his discussion of fictive histories, cyclical theories of history serve to familiarize the future, since they entail the repetition of patterns found in the past.[16] The theme of the rise and fall of civilizations has a powerful appeal to historically-minded writers; nevertheless, it deserves to be treated with some suspicion. The idea that civilizations reaching a certain stage *must* go into decline, though widespread in the post-Darwinian period, is a capitulation to anti-scientific irrationalism. Though the organic analogy for society is valid for some purposes, a society is not a living organism, any more than it is a factory for producing identical china dolls. The popular future histories based, for example, on Oswald Spengler's *The Decline of the West*,[17] express the fatalistic attitude that the future will be just like the past, if a bit more exotic – and there will be far, far more of it – rather than anything proper to scientific speculation.

Cyclical histories such as Asimov's *Foundation* trilogy (1951-3) and Walter M. Miller, Jr's *A Canticle for Leibowitz* (1959) typically consist of a series of disjointed episodes, each introducing a new set of characters and loosely tied together by an overall theme. In *A Canticle for Leibowitz*, for example, the theme is the Catholic church's survival and preservation of fragments of knowledge through the dark ages which succeed each epoch of scientific development. The novel ends with a second nuclear Armageddon on Earth, and the departure of a small group of monks in a spaceship. This closure of the cyclical history at a moment of destruction and possible new beginning is one way of ending such a story. Alternatively, as in Clarke's *Childhood's End* (1953), the story may lead up to a final mystical apocalypse. (Even the physicist J.D. Bernal indulges in such an apocalypse when, in his speculative essay *The World, the Flesh and the Devil*, he speaks of humanity 'becoming masses of atoms in space communicating by radiation, and ultimately perhaps resolving itself entirely into light'.[18]) Both cyclical repetition and ultimate mysticism are ways of shedding light on the 'black and blank' future and serve, in fact, as a means of extending the 'truncated epic' to what writers and publishers may consider a proper length. We have seen that evolutionism and technological determinism appear to speak to us with some certainty about the future, but in terms that are brief and cryptic in the extreme. At most, they suggest a number of crises that humanity is bound to confront in the future, while saying very little about the order and combination in which these crises will occur. The actual events are bound to be drastically modified by these contextual factors. I would suggest that these considerations have a bearing on the disappointing thinness of the 'heavyweight' histories (notably, those of Stapledon and Asimov) which have been cited. Conversely, they may also account for the excellence of some of SF's short stories. The epic strain in science fiction may be present to most advantage where a single future crisis is portrayed with precision and economy. In stories like Clarke's 'The Sentinel', Murray Leinster's 'First Contact', and Clifford D. Simak's 'Huddling Place', the possibilities of a future heroic age of space exploration are concentrated in the portrayal of a single future episode.

Robert A. Heinlein's early 'future history' series is a sequence of stories and novellas, some of which are merely trivial diversions and some of which present a serious view of future crises. The two culminating stories in the sequence, 'Universe' and 'Common Sense', despite the banalities of their literary style (they were first published in *Astounding Science Fiction* in 1941), are an effective portrayal of the relapse into barbarism following a mutiny aboard a spaceship on a 500-year voyage to Proxima Centauri. Several generations after the mutiny, a small group of men are able to defy the superstitious tyranny that has been established aboard the ship, and to recover the knowledge of the mission's nature and purpose. Though much in these stories (reprinted as *Orphans of the Sky*) will hardly bear re-reading, the hero's realization that there is a universe outside the ship, and his final landing with his followers on a virgin planet, fleetingly capture both the strangeness of seeing things for the first time that is essential to science fiction, and the noble simplicity that nineteenth-century critics associated with Homer. Here are the closing paragraphs of 'Common Sense':

> The sun had crossed a sizable piece of the sky, enough time had passed for a well-fed man to become hungry – and they were not well fed. Even the women were outside – that had been accomplished by the simple expedient of going back in and pushing them out. They had not ventured away from the side of the Ship, but sat huddled against it. But their menfolk had even learned to walk

singly, even in open spaces. Alan thought nothing of strutting a full fifty yards away from the shadow of the Ship, and did so more than once, in full sight of the women.

It was on one such journey that a small animal native to the planet let his curiosity exceed his caution. Alan's knife knocked him over and left him kicking. Alan scurried to the spot, grabbed his fat prize by one leg, and bore it proudly back to Hugh. 'Look, Hugh, look! Good eating!'

Hugh looked with approval. His first strange fright of the place had passed and had been replaced with a warm deep feeling, a feeling that he had come at last to his long home. This seemed a good omen.

'Yes', he agreed. 'Good eating. From now on, Alan, always Good Eating.'[19]

This is, of course, very transparent writing. One could go through it separating out the authentic primitivism of a new beginning in human history from the bogus, tribal primitivism of Heinlein's *macho* imagination. In addition, how lucky it is that this unsurveyed planet on which Hugh has made a blind landing just happens to be full of trees and juicy small animals! However, the 'ridiculous improbability' involved is something to which Heinlein carefully draws the reader's attention. He can afford to do so, much as Wells could afford the suggestion that the Time Traveller's adventures were no more than a made-up story. 'Common Sense' is a prophetic speculation about man's future which satisfies the epic requirements of realism, universality, heroic enterprise, and confrontation with forces beyond man's control. If 'Universe' and 'Common Sense' together make up a slim book of little over 120 pages, and if even at this length they contain a good deal of superfluous violent action, this should be taken as evidence that the one aspect of the traditional epic that science fiction does not inherit is its amplitude – except in the forms of romantic costume-drama and, perhaps, of parody.

Orphans of the Sky and similar works may be used to exem-

plify one of the classic modes of science fiction: the truncated epic based on the prospect of galactic imperialism,
with its associated themes of leaving the Earth, colonizing
the planets, and meeting with aliens. It remains to be noted
that early twentieth-century optimism about the conquest of
the universe has now receded, so that these themes can no
longer be successfully treated with the epic simplicity that
Heinlein found possible. The urge to write the epitaph of
the 'Space Age' is strong in such influential SF writers of the
1960s as Kurt Vonnegut, J.G. Ballard, and even Stanislaw
Lem. Both Vonnegut in *The Sirens of Titan* and Ballard in
many of his short stories offer deliberate parodies of the
future history. Ballard's 'Thirteen for Centaurus' is a neat
reversal of *Orphans of the Sky*, in which a precocious adolescent on board a multi-generational spaceship manages to
deduce, not only that there is a world outside the ship, but
that 'outside' is not deep space but a psychological laboratory on Earth. The simulated space voyage began as a
courageous experiment to provide the necessary data for
actual voyages; after two generations, during which public
opinion has decisively turned against the space programme,
it has turned into an embarrassing anachronism. As one of
the psychologists monitoring the experiment reflects, 'What
began as a grand adventure of the spirit of Columbus, has
become a grisly joke.'[20] The joke is not only at the expense of
the brainwashed crew – and of the psychologists who believe
that men can be kept in ignorance indefinitely – but of
galactic imperialism as a whole. In this and other stories
Ballard deliberately takes the form of the truncated epic
and turns it inside out.

When the old epics lost their primary authority over their
readers, they gave rise to the various modes of mock-epic,
comic epic, satire, and burlesque. Lucian's *True History*, the
earliest surviving narrative of interplanetary travel, begins
as a parody of the *Iliad* and the *Odyssey*. In recent years,
comic fantasy has become a prominent science-fictional
mode; one thinks not only of *The Sirens of Titan* but of
Calvino's *Cosmicomics* and of the seemingly inexhaustible

episodes of Lem's *The Cyberiad* and *The Star Diaries*. In addition, the representative SF novels of the 1960s and 1970s are, by and large, not future histories but stories of 'parallel worlds' created by changing or simply stepping outside man's actual historical world. Philip K. Dick's *The Man in the High Castle* and Kingsley Amis's *The Alteration* are well-known examples of this mode. While the spread of comic science fiction and the parallel-world story may reflect an increasingly sceptical attitude towards the scientific anticipations that fired an earlier generation of writers, the chief factor in their emergence is a growing self-consciousness about the conventions and language of SF. It is to the matter of language that we shall now turn.

6 IMITATION AND NOVELTY: AN APPROACH THROUGH SF LANGUAGE

L IKE some ageing space-freighter, the language of SF has usually been content to lumber along with its cargo of corn towards Lunarport Bathos. From an orthodox literary standpoint, science-fictional prose – especially that of the pulps – has been viewed with embarrassment, with fond condescension, and even with horror. It was not until the 1960s that there emerged a generation of SF novelists who were self-conscious stylists; before that time, one has to look to the occasional European writer, such as Zamyatin and Čapek, for the sense of linguistic experiment. The beginnings of the stylistic and semiotic analysis of the genre are still more recent.

Authenticity and the literary hoax

Up to and including Wells, science fiction was strongly influenced by the sober and impartial style of scientific statement which was first outlined by Bishop Sprat in his *History of the Royal Society* (1667). Soon 'scientific' plainness was taking the place of rhetorical ornamentation, both in realistic fiction and in the works now regarded as precursors of modern SF. The stylistic norm was no longer that of the 'tall tale' conscious of its own absurdity (as in Lucian's *True History* and Cyrano's *Voyages to the Moon and Sun*), but rather of authentic, eye-witness description. *Gulliver's Travels* and Holberg's *Journey of Niels Klim to the World Underground* (1741) provide examples of the new style, which Scott later found exemplified in *Frankenstein*:

It is no slight merit in our eyes, that the tale, though wild
in incident, is written in plain and forcible English, without exhibiting that mixture of hyperbolical Germanisms
with which tales of wonder are usually told, as if it were
necessary that the language should be as extravagant as
the fiction.[1]

Judged by standards other than those of the most sensational Gothic romances, *Frankenstein* now appears something less than the model of stylistic restraint that Scott
found it. Later writers, such as Poe (in some of his stories)
and Wells, try very much harder to achieve authenticity by
recounting the most extravagant incidents in 'plain and
forcible English'. Often they do this by deliberate imitation
of the deadpan styles of the travelogue, the ship's log-book,
the newspaper article, or the scientific report. Poe is a fan-
tasist whose imitations of the styles of 'objective' reporting
are never far from parody; Wells, more fundamentally convinced of the protean nature of the universe known to
science, is comparatively sober and restrained. The air of
authenticity which these writers cultivated led each to the
perpetration of a famous hoax – though, in Wells's case, this
was admittedly long-delayed and indirect. Poe's fictional
account of the first crossing of the Atlantic by balloon was
printed as a broadside by the *New York Sun* (13 April 1844),
and sold out so fast that its author himself was unable to
obtain a copy. Hundreds of thousands of listeners panicked
when Orson Welles's dramatization of *The War of the Worlds*
was broadcast over the CBS radio network in 1938. The
literary hoax is an extreme consequence of the imitation of
the factual styles of modern prose, and its natural habitat
seems to be the world of journalism. Poe's 'Balloon Hoax'
could only succeed in a world familiar with reports of bal-
loonists' feats, while Orson Welles made use of a simulated
newscast aimed at a public already jumpy with war-scares.
The stories that some newspapers print annually on 1 April
belong in the same general category. (The *Guardian* newspaper fooled many people on 1 April 1977 with its invention

of San Seriffe, an imaginary republic in the Indian Ocean – a somewhat science-fictional feat.) The ancestor of Poe and Wells as literary hoaxers is Daniel Defoe, whose *Robinson Crusoe* and *Journal of the Plague Year* are classics of illusory authenticity. *Crusoe*, at least, is closely allied to SF.

The language of novelty

The style of reportage, so adequate to describe that which is already familiar from experience, is severely handicapped when it comes to evoking the really new and strange. The virtue of 'plain and forcible English', in this context, can only be a virtue of understatement. (The Wellsian 'precision in the unessential and vagueness in the essential', as one early critic called it,[2] is an example of this.) The alternative is a rhetoric of emotive gestures toward the 'thrilling', the 'weird', the 'incredible', and the 'indescribable', which plays a major role in the Gothic novel and its derivatives, including *Frankenstein* and much of Poe. Twentieth-century 'hard' science fiction is concerned, by and large, with the authenticity of its visions and makes very sparing use of this sort of rhetoric. Understatement both of the novelty of what is seen and of the emotional reactions of the observer (an effect which tends to be accentuated by the very brief paragraphing characteristic of magazine SF) is just about the most reliable stylistic attribute of writers like Heinlein, Asimov, and Clarke. Here, taken almost at random, is the conclusion to chapter 33 of Clarke's *Rendezvous with Rama* (1973). The surgeon of the spaceship *Endeavour* is dissecting the first specimen of an alien life-form:

> The spider was so fragile that it almost came to pieces without her assistance. She disarticulated the legs, then started on the delicate carapace, which split along three great circles and opened up like a peeled orange.
>
> After some moments of blank incredulity – for there was nothing that she could recognize or identify – she took a series of careful photographs. Then she picked up her scalpel.

Where to start cutting? She felt like closing her eyes, and stabbing at random, but that would not have been very scientific.

The blade went in with practically no resistance. A second later, Surgeon-Commander Ernst's most unladylike yell echoed the length and breadth of *Endeavour*.

It took an annoyed Sergeant McAndrews a good twenty minutes to calm down the startled simps.[3]

The first three paragraphs here are dominated by a rhetoric of scientificity. Dr Ernst's 'moments of blank incredulity' are counteracted at once by the orderly procedures of science: 'She took a series of careful photographs.' Dr Ernst is doing her best to be 'very scientific', but her caution and discipline are to no avail. No seasoned reader of Anglo-American SF will be surprised by the sudden termination of the episode, or by the inadequacy of her 'most unladylike yell' to express what has really happened. The final two paragraphs might well be seen as exemplifying general conventions of magazine fiction (the punch-line/cliffhanger), but in fact they are specifically appropriate to the science-fictional nature of the text as well. Within the stylistic register of *Rendezvous with Rama*, Clarke could tell us what has caused Laura Ernst to cry out with pain (the 'spider' turned out to carry a strong electrical charge), but he could not find language to convey more immediately what it is, in that moment, that she has felt and seen. Later, of course, it will be rationally explained; the creature was a honeycomb of battery cells. The calculated change of focus in the final sentence assures us of some such regulatory outcome. What the style of reportage in science fiction habitually avoids is the sheer vividness of novel experience. Novelty, to such a style, is both its *raison d'être* and something it cannot confront directly.

In this passage the 'spider' is the source of a (literally) shocking alienness, but the 'simps' in Sergeant McAndrews' care are taken as a matter of course. (Simps, it has earlier been explained, are 'superchimps' or monkeys trained to perform menial tasks on board ship.) To the narrator – a future historian writing at an unspecified date, a good deal later than the year 2130 in which the story is set – there is nothing very odd or remarkable about the existence of simps. Here is a second way in which fantastic elements in a science-fiction story may be introduced with an air of prosaic verisimilitude. In *Rendezvous with Rama*, the temporal displacement of the narrator into the far future is very little emphasized. It is simply exploited to project the alien phenomena of the story against a background of interplanetary travel, communication, and political organization which can be taken for granted. The future historian speaks directly to us, and there is no suggestion that he might be an 'unreliable' narrator. A different technique, exemplified in stories such as Poe's 'Mellonta Tauta' and Zamyatin's *We*, uses a future narrator who is unreliable in the rather special sense that it is precisely the things he takes for granted which convey the alienness of his experience, and the difference between his assumptions and ours. In this writing there is no attempt to disguise the elements which signify novelty. Here, for example, is a brief episode from *We*. The narrator, D-503, has just met the woman who is to lure him into a posture of rebellion against the future totalitarian state:

> In parting, I-330 said with another of her X-smiles, 'Come to auditorium 112 the day after tomorrow.'
>
> I shrugged. 'If I am assigned to that auditorium. . .'
>
> And she, with an odd certainty, 'You will be.'
>
> The woman affected me as unpleasantly as an irresolvable irrational member that has somehow slipped into an equation. And I was glad to remain at least for a few moments alone with dear O.
>
> Hand in hand, we crossed four lines of avenues. At the corner she had to turn right, and I, left.
>
> 'I'd like so much to come to you today and let down the blinds. Today, right now . . .' O timidly raised her round, blue-crystal eyes to me.
>
> How funny she is. What could I say to her? She had come to me only the day before, and she knew as well as I

did that our next sexual day was the day after tomorrow. It was simply a case of her usual 'anticipative thought' – like the occasional (and sometimes damaging) premature supply of a spark to a motor.[4]

The permeation of nearly all aspects of Zamyatin's future state by mathematics is immediately evident from this extract, as is its attempted suppression of sexuality. I-330's charms are expressed through the medium of her 'X-smiles'; in fact every manifestation of female sexuality in the passage is characterized by its oddity, irrationality, and 'unpleasantness'. (As this is science fiction, we may be sure that this is a general feature of the society portrayed, rather than an individual quirk of D-503's.) O's very natural sexual responsiveness to the magnetism she has observed between her man and another woman is rebuffed by the narrator, not because his mind is engaged elsewhere, but because it is *not* 'natural' in a society in which privacy between two persons ('letting down the blinds') is only sanctioned in accordance with the timetable laid down by the state. D-503 is quite happy to remain 'alone with dear O' as long as it means no more than fulfilling the prescribed, and mathematical, public task – 'we crossed four lines of avenues'. However, while the surface level of the texts insists upon the novelty of the experience conveyed, we also see it as a new form of a very much more familiar and universal phenomenon – what is called, with an appropriately mathematical symbolism, the eternal triangle. D-503 finally does his best to reconcile O's unexpected spontaneity with his notions of order and regularity: 'It was simply a case of her usual "anticipative thought" – like the occasional (and sometimes damaging) premature supply of a spark to a motor.' The engineering simile 'explains' O's reaction in the terms of his world – and also, as it happens, of ours.

The absent signified

Recently certain critics have attempted to characterize the general category of science-fictional discourse, to which both the quoted extracts belong. In his essay 'About 5,750 Words' (1968), Samuel R. Delany urges that 'any serious discussion of speculative fiction must first get away from the distracting concept of s-f content and examine precisely what sort of word-beast sits before us'.[5] Delany's fullest examination of the word-beast is contained in one of the most remarkable critical books yet published on SF, *The American Shore* (1978). In this series of 'meditations on a tale of science fiction by Thomas M. Disch – *Angouleme*', Delany argues that the discourse of SF – unlike that of either realistic fiction or fantasy – is 'trivalent':

> The s-f text speaks inward, of course, as do the texts of mundane fiction, to create a subject (characters, plot, theme . . .). It also speaks outward to create a world, a world in dialogue with the real. And, of course, the real world speaks inward to construct its dialogue with both. But as there *are* three different discourses involved, there is really no way any two of the three *can* be congruent, or even complementary, to the other. At best, the s-f writer harmonizes them.[6]

The trivalency of SF, then, arises from the gap between the hypothetical 'world' within which the narrative events are located, and the everyday empirical world. This is true of all fiction to some extent; for example, Delany in a more recent essay cites the case of the historian reading Jane Austen and realizing that her world is 'completely different from the world as it actually was back then'.[7] SF, unlike fantasy, refers to a possible world and, at the same time, dispels any illusion that that world might be identifiable with the real one. Where the imagined world and the empirical world do appear to coincide, it might be added, the author does not allow us to experience the pleasures of congruence for long. Instead, he is lying in wait to ambush us with the disturbingly unfamiliar – and, in all probability, relishing his hoax.

From a more orthodox semiotic point of view, Marc Angenot describes the reference made by every science-fiction text to a non-empirical, hypothetical reality as involving an 'absent paradigm'.[8] In the passage from *Rendezvous with Rama* quoted above, for example, at least four textual items act to signify the strangeness of what is being described:

> the delicate carapace, which split along three great circles (i)
> there was nothing that she could recognize or identity (ii)
> Surgeon-Commander Ernst's most unladylike yell (iii)
> to calm down the startled simps (iv)

Items (ii) and (iii) are negatives, indicating no more than the presence of the unexpected. Items (i) and (iv) define the science-fictional world with which we are concerned. 'Simps', and all other invented words in SF, Angenot contends, are not neologisms but 'fictive words'. They differ from the fictive words of nonsense literature in that they imply a consistent (though absent) linguistic paradigm – in this case, the language-world of Clarke's AD 2130. The spider's carapace 'split along three great circles', we come to learn, because it was artifically constructed in accordance with the rule of 'Rama redundancy'; every Raman artefact appears to be replicated in threes. This 'rule of three' is a fictive scientific theory entertained by Clarke's human characters, whose contact with Raman civilization remains somewhat premature. (For example, it is not explained why Rama has not three but six artificial suns.) The rule of three is no more than a sign of the *possibility* of a rational understanding of Raman civilization.

Where aliens in a science-fiction novel engage in direct communication, we are presented not only with hypotheses about an extraterrestrial nature ('exobiology') but with an extraterrestrial linguistics. The possession of a non-human language is, indeed, the fundamental distinguishing-mark of 'alien intelligence'. It has been far more common in SF to refer to the existence of such languages (which may very well not involve spoken communication) than to attempt to describe or transcribe them. In many 'first contact' stories it is simply supposed that all difficulties of mutual comprehension are over once the technicians have set up their translating machines. Actual verbal representations of alien language present a fascinating, if as yet somewhat restricted, area of study. Such representations can only be based on the controlled distortion of the writer's own language, to produce either a phonetic rendering or a translation of the alien language. The result may be words which appear to be gibberish (transliteration) or a heavily stylized dialect (translation). Setting aside words of future English, such as Orwell's 'doublethink', Heinlein's Martian verb 'to grok' (from *Stranger in a Strange Land*) is probably the only genuinely alien fictive word which has passed into colloquial usage.

SF novels do not have to contain either fictive words or invented languages; these are merely particular manifestations of the genre's reference to an altered and hypothetical, rather than an empirical, reality. Angenot describes the manner of this reference as follows:

> The SF narrative always assumes a 'not-said' that regulates the message. The rhetoric of credibility aims at having the reader believe not so much in what is literally said as in what is assumed or presupposed. Emphasis is not placed primarily on the characters and events of the future or extraterrestrial world but on types, models, norms, and institutions that are only summarily and allusively represented by these characters and events.[9]

The trivalency of science-fictional discourse, to use Delany's term, results from the distance between the 'not-said' of an SF novel and the empirical world which constitutes the 'not-said' of realism.

Intertextuality and parody

Delany describes the relationship between the imaginary world of SF and the empirical world as one of dialogue. This dialogue is, of course, mediated by many factors; indeed, the existence of complex linguistic and structural relationships between the two worlds is required if it is to take place intelligibly at all. The use of conventions and stereotypes in science fiction that was discussed in chapter 3 forms part of a wider phenomenon, that of intertextual reference, which substantially qualifies the autonomy of the paradigmatic world set up by each individual text. Michel Butor has suggested in a controversial essay that SF writers should collaborate in developing a 'collective myth' of the future which would exert a constraining power over the individual writer's imagination.[10] In fact, it might be argued that SF once had a 'collective myth', and has since lost it. Readers in the heyday of the magazines (roughly 1930–60), according to T.A. Shippey, appreciated 'cross-references, argument, parody, in an almost subliminal way'.[11] It is well known that academic critics of this 'collective mode' are inclined to credit a given idea or story with greater originality than it really possesses; similarly, ignorance of the magazine context may blind them to some of the subtleties of a story's development. The high productivity among writers addressing a closed and 'addicted' readership led to the constant borrowing and alteration of one another's themes. The thematic indexes and surveys compiled by SF scholars enable one to trace this practice, although they themselves are rarely concerned to generalize about it. More recently, SF novelists have tended to approach the 'collective myth' of the genre – such as it is – in a spirit of self-conscious imitation and parody.

For example, one may consider the literary diaspora belonging to Wells's *War of the Worlds* (1898) – a diaspora which extends, at its outer edges, to every twentieth-century narrative of invasion from outer space. There are a number of adaptations, both acknowledged and unacknowledged, of Wells's story, beginning with pirated versions in the American yellow press, and including radio and film versions. Then there are imitations and 'sequels' such as George H. Smith's *The Second War of the Worlds* (1976), which deals with an invasion of a second planet by Wells's identical creatures. Next comes the vast number of stories describing the disruption of human society by an alien force: novels

like John Wyndham's *The Day of the Triffids* (1951) and
Ursula Le Guin's *The Lathe of Heaven* (1971), which confess
varying degrees of Wellsian influence but all belong to the
sub-genre which *The War of the Worlds* orginates. Finally,
there are conscious examples of parody and pastiche. Christopher Priest's *The Space Machine* (1976) is dedicated to
Wells and sends its 1890s hero and heroine on a trip to the
red planet, where they find themselves mixed up with the
Martian invasion fleet. In sharp contrast to this gentle pastiche is Arkady and Boris Strugatsky's novella 'The Second
Martian Invasion' (1968), in which the Martians successfully
exploit the creeping bureaucratic techniques of contemporary tyranny. The point of this satire by the two leading
Soviet SF writers lies precisely in the distance between the
Strugatskys' Martians (who remain unseen, but employ
humanoid robots to collect gastric juices from the docile
inhabitants of a village far from the battlefront) and their
bloody and apocalyptic Wellsian forebears.

For a full-blown parody of the 'Martian invasion' theme,
one must turn to Kurt Vonnegut, Jr's *The Sirens of Titan*
(1959). In Vonnegut's novel the army of Mars, under the
direction of the chrono-synclastically-infundibulated Winston Niles Rumfoord, mounts a feeble attack upon Earth
which is countered with the utmost brutality. The terrestrial
victory is followed by guilt and revulsion and the founding
of a new religion – all events which turn out to have been
stage-managed by Rumfoord himself. These are only two
episodes in the complex plot of a novel which is not so much
a parody of Wells, or of any individual SF author, as of the
genre as a whole. Vonnegut began as a relatively 'straight'
science-fiction author in *Player Piano* (1952), and has since
acquired an international reputation as a postmodernist
comedian of the absurd in novels like *Slaughterhouse-Five*
(1970) and *Breakfast of Champions* (1973). In view of his later
reputation, it may be necessary to insist that – despite its
metaphysical dimension – *The Sirens of Titan* is fundamentally a witty and inventive fantasy or 'tall tale' debunking

most aspects of the 'collective myth' of earlier science fiction.

Two of Vonnegut's main targets, as might be expected, are the future history and galactic imperialism. In *The Sirens of Titan* it is revealed that the whole purpose of man's history (to the extent, at least, that it culminates in space-travel) is to produce a spare part for a Tralfamadorian spaceship grounded on Titan. The spaceship (like Mariner IV) is carrying a message to the far side of the universe. Eventually we learn that the message consists of a single dot, which in Tralfamadorian means 'Greetings'. From a human viewpoint, Vonnegut's narrator condemns the utter pointlessness of space exploration, which leads to a 'nightmare of meaninglessness without end'.[12] The central symbol of this nightmare is Rumfoord, imprisoned, Cheshire cat-like, with his dog Kazak in one of the chrono-synclastic infundibula which put an end to man's first attempts at journeying into space. This concept, a parody of serious science, is explained to the reader by means of an extract from *A Child's Cyclopedia of Wonders and Things to Do* – a travesty of SF's normal conventions of scientific explanation.

Apart from space-travel, the science most persistently parodied in *The Sirens of Titan* is that of communications. Countless aspects of the novel, from the verbal wit of the chapter headings to the eighteen imaginary books and articles quoted by the narrator, reflect Vonnegut's own self-consciousness about language and the uncertain relationship of sign to meaning. Contemporary structuralism and semiotics teach us to look upon all cultural artefacts as coded messages; communications theory adds that all messages presuppose a sender and a receiver. If the history of human civilization is the 'message', who could possibly be sending it, and to whom? Vonnegut's Tralfamadorian hypothesis is no more absurd than any other. But how much energy and wastefulness is involved in attempts to communicate even the simplest message!

Old Salo had watched many communications failures on

Earth. Civilizations would start to bloom on Earth, and the participants would start to build tremendous structures that were obviously to be messages in Tralfamadorian – and then the civilizations would poop out without having finished the messages.[13]

The flatness of Vonnegut's style comes from its parodying of a language that is already flat; 'communications failures' is standard technologese. The brief paragraphing which is a feature of this novel is taken directly from the SF magazines. Vonnegut's deliberate use of bathos might be compared to Clarke's, in the *Rendezvous with Rama* passage quoted above. Yet, for Vonnegut, this usually involves a brutal debunking of the scientific vision. Typical, for example, is Salo's statue of a laboratory-gowned scientist, 'without vanity, without lust', engaged in the discovery of atomic power: 'And then one perceived that the young truth-seeker had a shocking erection.'[14] At the human level *The Sirens of Titan* traces, with admiration and mockery, the blind efforts of Malachi Constant, the 'faithful messenger', to remain true to himself in a universe which is alternately characterized as a clockwork machine and a junkyard. And, just as these two metaphors suggest the two faces of nineteenth-century cosmology – the 'universe rigid' dictated by natural laws and the entropic universe of the laws of thermodynamics – Vonnegut's novel as a whole gains its coherence and artistic validity from its pervasive debunking of earlier SF and the world-view which sustained it.

Entropy and disintegration

However bizarre the events of *The Sirens of Titan*, they all take place within the confines of a consistent, 'knowable' fictional world. The meaning of human experiences is constantly questioned, but the reality of those experiences within the fictional construct is never in doubt. In this respect, Vonnegut's portrayal of the breakdown of the scientific vision falls short of that of other contemporary novelists, for whom the sense of reality itself appears increasingly delusive and threatening. Like Vonnegut's comedy of the absurd, the fiction of the paranoid vision today spans both the 'mainstream' and the science-fiction categories. In science fiction, its representative (and highly prolific) exponent is Philip K. Dick.

One of Dick's favourite narrative techniques is to contrast 'normal' perception with what is seen as the essentially truer and more clairvoyant experience of the psychotic or schizophrenic. The description of weird psychic states is, of course, one of the oldest preoccupations of science fiction and fantasy. Many of Wells's short stories, for example, are based on parapsychological phenomena for which a scientific explanation may or may not be offered. Dick and other contemporary novelists go much further than this, presenting a 'post-scientific' view of reality which threatens to undermine the whole basis and value-system on which scientific observation is built. Like many of his novels, *Martian Time-Slip* (1964) is set in a mildly dystopian future (the date is 1994), in which scientific advances have failed to bring about the human emancipation they once promised. The settlement of the bleak landscape of Mars has brought few obvious benefits to mankind, and the settlers are given over to profiteering and land-speculation among themselves and to oppression of the native inhabitants. Meanwhile, they are troubled by the growing incidence of schizophrenia and other psychic abnormalities among them. A new theory explains schizophrenia as a derangement in the interior time-sense, which sometimes involves precognition. The story concerns the attempt of a Martian tycoon to harness the precognitive powers of Manfred, an autistic boy, in order to aid his investments. But what Manfred sees in the future is a nightmare of mechanization leading to universal decay; a world in which the human being is a 'tangle of pumps and hoses and dials', while the world he creates and even the language he uses are a jumble of garbage and nonsense. This is the world of 'absolute reality',[15] manifesting the hidden meaning of modern attempts to subdue nature and to conquer the universe. The only possibility of salvation lies with the dying tribes of Martian natives – the Bleekmen – whose religious 'superstitions' are a means of harnessing precognitive powers and turning them to human advantage.

Martian Time-Slip is most likely to be read as an anti-capitalist, anti-imperialist fable, in which the science-fictional plot centring upon theories of autism and schizophrenia is a little clumsily handled. One of the novel's most interesting features, however, is its verbal representation of these 'precognitive' modes of experience. In chapters 10 and 11, three alternative descriptions of the same episode are used to convey the sense of mental breakdown. Each replay of the scene is introduced by the same three sentences:

> Inside Mr Kott's skin were dead bones, shiny and wet. Mr Kott was a sack of bones, dirty and yet shiny-wet. His head was a skull that took in greens and bit them; inside him the greens became rotten things as something ate them to make them dead.[16]

The verbal repetition and the unstated point of view force the reader to share some of the mental confusion of Dick's characters. Until this confusion is rationally explained – which happens two chapters later – the reader's sense of the unified nature of the fictional world is profoundly disturbed. In more recent novels such as *Ubik* (1970) and *A Scanner Darkly* (1977), Dick has further developed this disintegrative technique.

Dick's handling of the theme of precognition in *Martian Time-Slip* inverts the premises of a scientific future in a way that is characteristic of a large amount of contemporary SF. Not only does galactic imperialism distressingly parallel earthly imperialism, but the two main sources of 'rational' prophecy – technological determinism and evolutionism – are sardonically exploited to show the hopelessness of man's historical and biological situation. Technological determinism leads to the nightmare of a world of machines which is a stereotyped parody of the human world. In *Martian Time-Slip* this is epitomized by Jack Bohlen's visit to the Public School, where he finds his mental stability threatened by the lifelikeness of the teaching machines. Evolutionism, on the other hand, leads only to the nightmare of entropy – of the running-down universe in which everything is falling into disuse and decay:

> All Mars, [Kott] decided, was a sort of Humpty Dumpty; the original state had been one of perfection, and they and their property had all fallen from that state into rusty bits and useless debris. He felt sometimes as if he presided over an enormous junkyard.[17]

It need hardly be added that neither Kott nor anyone else is destined to rule in this junkyard for very long. Manfred's autism, we come to realize, is an enforced silence in the face of his own ghastly vision of universal decay. The scientific preoccupation with the future appears in *Martian Time-Slip* as a manic disruption of the decencies and reticences of daily living, whether these are located in the civilization of the Bleekman, in the spartan lives of the frontier settlers, or in the silence of the mentally ill.

In Dick's novels, then, the disintegration of the scientific vision is reflected in the partial disintegration of the imagined world. The novel 'speaks outward', in Delany's terms, to create not one but several possible subjective worlds, which it brings into dialogue with one another as well as with the 'real' world. The elements of parody and satire in these novels testify to their genetic descent from earlier science fiction. The fiction of Vonnegut and Dick is a sign either of the dissolution or the renovation of SF; at all events, it is a response to the changing nature of scientific thought and of our notions of 'reality' itself. Quantum theory, with its concept of the wave which is also a particle, may lead to a wider notion of the reversibility of what were once inviolable categories: thus, in various recent SF novels, outer space turns into 'inner space', while science – in such books as Miller's *A Canticle for Leibowitz* and John Boyd's *The*

Last Starship from Earth – turns into religion. This reversibility of categories often turns on a joke; in Boyd's novel, for instance, the 'last starship' turns out to have been the one that Christ caught on Ascension Day. In this and many other contemporary examples, the entropy and disintegration which threaten to undermine the scientific world-view are expressed in fiction which itself tends toward the condition of parody.

Romance, fable, epic, and parody: Lem's *Solaris*

A classic work might be defined as one which embodies all the potentialities of the genre to which it belongs. The intensive reading of such a work will, in effect, be a rehearsal of all that the genre is and might be. The 'classic' label has been very freely bandied about in SF – from Asimov's *Foundation* to Zelazny's *Lord of Light* – but this is a sign of a shortage rather than an abundance of agreed classics. Perhaps only Wells's *The Time Machine* has been universally accepted as a generic masterpiece by writers, readers, critics, and theorists. It is too early to say whether Stanislaw Lem's *Solaris* (1961) is on its way to such widespread acceptance. It may, however, serve as a culmination to the present discussion, since it displays originality along each of the four generic axes that have been discussed in this book. Lem himself may still be in need of introduction to English-speaking readers, although, thanks largely to the circulation of his books throughout the Eastern bloc as well as in his native Poland, he is (to say the least) one of the most widely-read SF authors in the world. His diverse production ranges from conventional SF novels such as *The Astronauts* (1951) to the comic fables of *The Cyberiad* (1965), as well as to philosophical writings on cybernetics and literary theory. *Solaris*, written at the mid-point of his career, has reached its widest audience in the West through Andrei Tarkovsky's somewhat freely-adapted Soviet film version. The novel itself, unfortunately, is as yet only available in English in a translation based on the French translation of the Polish original. Nevertheless, *Solaris*, I would claim, is a science-fictional classic because it exemplifies the creative fusion of romance, fable, epic, and parody.

The surface of the planet Solaris is covered by an ocean, made of some colloidal substance, which is perpetually in motion and has the property of assuming endless, unrepeated shapes. Generations of scientists have come to study the ocean, which they believe to be some sort of intelligent organism. Gradually they have become obsessed with the humanistic, almost religious, aim of 'Contact' with it. Throughout the history of Solaristic studies, no communication has ever been achieved. All that has happened is that a few scientists and explorers have disappeared in unexplained circumstances. Lem's novel is framed by a sort of interrupted space voyage. It begins with the hero, Kelvin, leaving the mother-ship *Prometheus* to make his descent towards Solaris, and ends with him landing for the first time on the planet's surface. The main narrative describes his experiences during the months that he spends on the research station hovering over the ocean. Arriving at the station, he finds two of his distinguished colleagues, Sartorius and Snow, in what seems a state of extreme paranoia, while a third, Gibarian, has committed suicide that morning. The upheaval at the station has been caused by the Visitors – products, apparently, of the latest stage in the ocean's attempts to make Contact with mankind. Its emissaries take the form of human simulacra, often but not necessarily women, synthesized by the ocean on the basis of its intensive 'brain-scanning' of the memories and secret obsessions of the individuals destined to receive them. The Visitors are programmed to stay with their hosts at all times, and they are capable of extraordinary violence under the panic induced by separation. The plasma of their bodies is self-healing, and when definitely got rid of (locked into a rocket-ship, for example, and blasted into orbit) they are simply replaced by new versions after a few hours. They are of normal intelligence and have, at first, no inkling of their extraterrestrial origin.

The generic elements of *Solaris* may be isolated as follows:

1 romance: the story of the Visitors – Gothic narrative tinged with erotic sensationalism and horror;

2 fable: the problem of Contact, revealing the epistemological limitations of scientific thought when confronting alien intelligence;

3 epic: Kelvin's journey as space voyager, his attempts to solve the riddle of Solaris and take his place in the line of 'great Solarists', and his eventual landing on the planet and decision to stay there;

4 parody: the imaginary science of Solaristics, its language and concepts, its history, and its apparent futility. Conventional scientific attitudes and habits of thought when confronted by the test-case of the apparently insoluble.

Romance in *Solaris* is twofold. The Visitors are, for the most part, embodiments of private sexual or infantile obsessions: exotic stereotypes such as the negress who drove Gibarian to suicide and the dwarf which cohabits with Sartorius. Life with these creatures is a nightmare of shame and horror, exemplified by Sartorius' secretiveness, Gibarian's suicide, and the mysterious bloodstains on Snow's hands. At first, Snow treats Kelvin as a possible Visitor, receiving him not with fraternal warmth but with open and unfeigned terror. If these elements belong to a mystery story, Kelvin's own dilemma is the opposite of that of his colleagues. His Visitor, Rheya, is a reconstruction of an actual person with whom he once had a disastrous love-affair. Inevitably he becomes infatuated with her, despite his 'scientific' understanding of the impossibility of such a relationship. The ending of this doomed and tainted love-relationship is, perhaps, predictable. Once Snow and Sartorius have perfected a device for destabilizing the neutrino structure of which the Visitors are composed, Rheya, like her terrestrial counterpart, commits suicide. Her disappearance leaves Kelvin with a much stronger emotional commitment to 'seeing through' the Solaris mystery than have his colleagues.

Lem's opening sentence – 'At 19.00 hours, ship's time, I made my way to the launching bay'[18] – establishes *Solaris* within the class of 'space epics'. Yet it is pastiche and parody rather than the straight epic mode which come to the fore in the long passages in which Kelvin reconstructs the history and methodology of the science of Solaristics. Much of his time is spent in the library at the centre of the research station. It is as if the secrets of Solaris are contained in the scientific literature rather than in the raw phenomena which can be seen through the portholes. The 'ocean of Solaris', Lem writes at one point, 'was submerging under an ocean of printed paper'.[19] Lem's descriptions of the science of Solaristics are an astonishing achievement. Throughout these accounts of the phenomena to be studied – the 'mimoids', 'extensors', 'symmetriads' and other plastic forms thrown up by the ocean – and of the theories that have grown up around them there runs a sense of futility, the feeling that 'we had not progressed an inch in the 78 years since researches had begun'.[20] The fundamental obstacle to progress is the anthropomorphism of scientific theories, caricatured in the popular views of Solaris as the 'cosmic yogi', the 'autistic ocean', or even the 'planet in orgasm'. Lem does not hold out much hope that this anthropomorphism, which presumably applies to all science, can ever be surmounted.

The history of Solaristics that he gives would remind Anglo-American readers of Thomas Kuhn's book *The Structure of Scientific Revolutions* (though the priority seems to lie with Lem, since Kuhn came out in 1962). In Kelvin's lifetime Solaristics has declined from a dynamic field full of conflicting theories to a steady accumulation of specialized and apparently meaningless data. The discipline has fragmented, so that it seems symbolically apt that Kelvin, Sartorius, and Snow, a psychologist, a physicist, and a cyberneticist respectively, spend most of their time locked in their

cabins unwilling or unable to communicate with each other.
Moreover, Lem shows that the only real insights into the
nature of Solaris have been ignored or officially hushed up
because they failed to fit into the prevailing assumptions as
to what was 'objective' and 'scientific'. The early stages of the
ocean's 'Operation Man', which led to the production of the
Visitors, had in fact been observed by a pilot whose tes-
timony was condemned as subjective and hallucinatory.
Kelvin and Snow discuss whether they are better off
marooned on the station, or requesting help from Earth
which will inevitably result in their being committed to a
mental hospital. Not only are explorers who have the courage of their own observations suspected of insanity, but the
only theorists who have got near to the truth about Solaristics have been dismissed as eccentrics, pseudo-scientists, and
cranks.

Kelvin comes to realize that this 'science' which excludes
any data which do not fit its preordained schemes is really
only a kind of mythology. It is anthropomorphic because
based on a set of assumptions which are helpless to comprehend the real alienness of Solaris. Searching in the hope
of enlightenment among the so-called lunatic fringe of Solarists, Kelvin discovers the pamphlets of Muntius, who
maintained that Solaristics had become 'the space era's
equivalent of religion', and of Grastrom who

> set out to demonstrate that the most abstract achieve-
> ments of science, the most advanced theories and vic-
> tories of mathematics represented nothing more than a
> stumbling, one or two-step progression from our rude,
> prehistoric, anthropomorphic understanding of the uni-
> verse around us. He pointed out correspondences with
> the human body – the projections of our senses, the
> structure of our physical organization, and the physiolog-
> ical limitations of man – in the equations of the theory of
> relativity, the theorem of magnetic fields and the various
> unified field theories. Grastrom's conclusion was that
> there neither was, nor could be, any question of 'contact'
> between mankind and any nonhuman civilization.[21]

In rehabilitating such views, Kelvin is rewriting the history of Solaristics in the Kuhnian sense, in accordance with the new paradigm emerging from the experience of the Visitors. What were previously classed as apocrypha, as pseudo-scientific outbursts from the lunatic fringe, are now coming to form the main text. But this 'text' is one that illustrates the circularity of scientific theories and the self-enclosed nature of the institutions within which they arise. Within the novel, the self-parodying tendencies of scientific behaviour and ideology are represented by the figure of Sartorius, the punctilious physicist who addresses Kelvin 'as though he were in the chair at the Institute'.[22] When they have decided to beam Kelvin's encephalograph at the ocean in a last, desperate attempt to put a stop to the visitations, Sartorius outlines a series of topics for him to consider during the recording session. Sartorius' pompous little speech neatly underlines the smugness of scientific ideology:

> Earth and Solaris; the body of scientists considered as a single entity, although generations succeed each other and man as an individual has a limited span; our aspirations, and our perseverance in the attempt to establish an intellectual contact; the long historic march of humanity, our own certitude of furthering that advance, and our determination to renounce all personal feelings in order to accomplish our mission; the sacrifices that we are prepared to make, and the hardships we stand ready to overcome . . . These are the themes that might properly occupy your awareness. The association of ideas does not depend entirely on your own will. However, the very fact of your presence here bears out the authenticity of the progression I have drawn to your attention.[23]

Kelvin's response to this is to think during the recording of Rheya, of Giese ('the father of Solarist studies'), and of his own father. It is their existence that explains his individual 'presence' at the station.

Since scientific ideology is the theme of *Solaris*, Sartorius' speech involves not only the element of parody but the element of fable. *Solaris* is, in effect, a dramatization of a position of epistemological scepticism which is common to many of Lem's other works. The anthropomorphic basis of all human thought seems to preclude any certainty as to the ocean's purpose in creating the Visitors. All that can be done is to add to the vast midden-heap of Solarist hypotheses already in existence. The success of the X-ray transmission implies that the ocean was not motivated by malice, simply by a failure to grasp the emotional torture it was inflicting on its human victims; Snow hypothesizes that 'Perhaps it was sending us . . . presents'.[24] Both Kelvin and Snow toy with the religious idea of Solaris as the manifestation of an 'imperfect God' – perhaps an infantile one. Lem's novel, however, is more than a philosophical parable, since it dramatizes the social basis as well as the metaphysical implications of these ideas. The Solaris research station is, as Sartorius points out, an embodiment of the scientific ethos of cosmic expansion and impersonal self-sacrifice; that is, it reflects a commitment to devote immense resources to the restless pursuit of abstract knowledge of the natural universe – resources which, we must assume, could have been put to other uses nearer home. Sartorius, Snow, and Kelvin represent three aspects of the breed of 'scientific man' – the intellectual élite whom a society capable of giving birth to Solaristics is geared to produce. Sartorius is responsible both for the destabilizer which kills off the Visitors, and for the X-ray bombardment of the ocean which transgresses a UN convention. Driven on by inscrutable private obsessions, he is the weapons technologist whose one virtue is that he 'gets results'. Snow's liberalism is, in the end, a helpless scepticism; he cannot change his colleagues' actions but can only hint to them that the craze for space exploration represents a massive evasion of man's real problems. His destructive criticism of the others does not disguise his own intellectual and moral defeat. Kelvin, ironically dubbed by Snow a 'Knight of the Holy Contact', is a romantic idealist, imaginative, open to experience, and convinced that confrontation with the mysteries of Solaris is for him a personal mission. His mental isolation from Sartorius and Snow is indicative both of the blind folly of his love for Rheya, and of the qualities which may be destined to make him the last of the great Solarists who have made fundamental discoveries about the ocean – assuming, that is, that such discoveries have been made at all. His final decision to stay on Solaris may be read as the sign either of romantic delusion or of genius.

Considered as a fable or parable, *Solaris* is 'open-ended'.[25] Another way of putting this would be to say that it presents one episode from a history whose outcome cannot be foreseen. At its conclusion, the novel reverts to a tentative version of the epic mode in which it began. Protesting that he does not wish to be welcomed home as a 'Solarist who has never set foot on Solaris', Kelvin leaves the space station for the first time and lands on the planet's surface. Once he has landed on the shore of an 'old mimoid' surrounded by the ocean he knows that he will not return to Earth, at least until some sequel to the experience with Rheya has been granted to him. Such is Kelvin's way of facing up to the 'totality of [his] existence, as his father and Giese had once done'.[26] He comes to it as, standing on the shore, he stretches out his hand to play a peculiar game of 'handshaking' with the ocean:

> What followed was a faithful reproduction of a phenomenon which had been analyzed a century before: the wave hesitated, recoiled, then enveloped my hand without touching it, so that a thin covering of 'air' separated my glove inside a cavity which had been fluid a moment previously, and now had a fleshy consistency. I raised my hand slowly, and the wave, or rather an outcrop of the wave, rose at the same time, enfolding my hand in a translucent cyst with greenish reflections. I stood up, so as to raise my hand still higher, and the gelatinous substance stretched like a rope, but did not break. . . . I repeated the game several times, until – as

the first experimenter had observed – a wave arrived which avoided me indifferently, as if bored with a too familiar sensation. I knew that to revive the 'curiosity' of the ocean I would have to wait several hours. Disturbed by the phenomenon I had stimulated, I sat down again. Although I had read numerous accounts of it, none of them had prepared me for the experience as I had lived it, and I felt somehow changed.[27]

Kelvin decides to remain on Solaris, in the hope that the 'Contact' he has experienced will be renewed. The continuity of Solaristics is guaranteed by this heroic – and quite possibly foolhardy – decision; all that is left is to see what his place in that history will be.

'I knew nothing, and I persisted in the faith that the time of cruel miracles was not past.'[28] If these closing words set the seal on the epic mode in *Solaris*, they also indicate that the subject of the novel is one of fundamental and unresolved mystery. For all that we have learned of its myriad phenomena, the ocean of Solaris is as enigmatic at the end of Lem's novel as it was at the beginning. Science fiction can show few more powerful embodiments of the novelty – the *new thing* – on which this fictional genre is based. The direct confrontation with the utterly novel could only lead to a Wittgensteinian impasse; Gibarian's conclusion that 'Where there are no men, there cannot be motives accessible to men'[29] seems to echo the conclusion of *Tractatus Logico-Philosophicus* (1921) that 'Whereof we cannot speak, thereof must we remain silent'. Man, however, must find ways of speaking of that which is novel, and he does so by imitation and recombination of the modes of discourse already at his command. Science fiction provides a particular instance of this, building up its stories of the new and strange by instituting a dialogue with what we already know. In this complex construction that is the SF story we may find bound together – as steel, concrete, wood, and glass may be bound together – the elements of romance, fable, epic, and parody.

7 THE SCIENCE-FICTION COURSE

As far as is known, the first college SF course was taught by Sam Moskowitz at the City College of New York in 1953.[1] The first to have any impact in educational circles was Mark R. Hillegas' course, which began at Colgate in 1962. Five years later, Hillegas, who was now at Southern Illinois University, published an article reflecting somewhat dispiritedly on his experiences as an SF teacher. Despite a predominantly 'mainstream' list of texts, including *Brave New World, Nineteen Eighty-Four, Lord of the Flies*, and several Wells titles, Hillegas reported growing opposition from his faculty colleagues. Given the conservatism of literary intellectuals and the anti-scientific bias of English departments, he concluded, there was 'no future for a course in science fiction'.[2]

Few prophets – let alone scholars in the field of utopian and anti-utopian literature – can have been disproved more quickly. By 1976 there were estimated to be around 2,000 college-level courses in SF in the United States, or at least one course for every college and university in the country.[3] It was not unusual for a major university English department to run two courses concurrently – one for freshmen and one for seniors – as well as training graduate teaching assistants in the subject and sponsoring the occasional PhD. Other departments which might offer science fiction as part of their curriculum ranged from sociology to physics. Nobody bothered to survey the spread of courses at high-school level, but the production of text-books, anthologies, and advisory material for prospective teachers was becoming a major industry. Though there is (at the time of writing) no Chair of Science-Fiction Studies, academic careers and reputations have already been made in the field. Nevertheless, Hillegas' cautious view of the future of the subject was not wholly unjustified. In particular, science fiction has as yet made comparatively little progress at British colleges and universities, despite the leading role that contemporary British writers play in the genre. The reasons for this are mostly to be sought in the less democratic, less consumer-oriented, and more narrowly specialist character of British higher education. The social pressures which, in the late 1960s and early 1970s, virtually overwhelmed the curricular conservatism of English departments in the United States and Canada have been much less urgently felt in Britain, where – at a rough guess – somewhere between a dozen and twenty universities and polytechnics, together with the occasional adult education centre, may now be offering a science-fiction course.

The 'two-cultures' debate and the student revolution

One of the factors influencing the spread of SF courses is, undoubtedly, the so-called 'two cultures' debate of the early 1960s. C.P. Snow's 1959 Rede Lecture, *The Two Cultures and the Scientific Revolution*, echoed the arguments of earlier scientific educators such as T.H. Huxley and H.G. Wells that the predominance of arts subjects in the educational system left school-leavers and graduates dangerously unfitted for life in the modern world. Snow's trenchant but slightly patronizing argument met with a violent counter-blast from the literary critic F.R. Leavis, who poured scorn on the idea that knowledge of the Second Law of Thermodynamics could somehow be equivalent to knowledge of a work of Shakespeare's. At the level of high intellectual debate, the passions generated by Snow and Leavis, and their refusal or inability to engage with one another on mutually compatible terms, made the whole controversy rather futile. As rival pronouncements on educational policy, however, there is no doubt that Snow's and (to a lesser extent) Leavis's ideas were listened to. Snow served as a Minister in the 1964 Labour administration, which was responsible for such measures as the creation of 'technological universities' and the greatly increased participation of scientific and economic advisers in government. Leavis, on the other hand, offered an out-and-out opposition to the ruling 'technologico-Benthamite' ideology. His appeal to teachers and students was a portent of the emotional revulsion against the modern state apparatus which, in the late 1960s, swept across the campuses of America and Europe.

For the literary teacher shamed by Snow into awareness of his and his pupils' ignorance of science and technology, science fiction was a natural place to turn to. (Martin Green's *Science and the Shabby Curate of Poetry*, published in 1963, is the record of one such 'conversion'.) But, given the low literary level of the average SF novel at this time, such a gesture could lead to rapid disillusionment. Scientific writers were often as contemptuous of the genre as their literary counterparts. Here, for example, is the Harvard biochemist William S. Beck, in his popular survey of *Modern Science and the Nature of Life* (1957):

> Scientists sometimes note wistfully that the huge and obvious reservoir of cordial interest in science among readers of books so often finds its outlet in science fiction, a genre of writing that is lately showing alarming signs of taking itself seriously. The pity of it is that *nothing* in SF – from the Mutants loose among the galaxies to the trans-Aristotelian world of *Null-A* – nothing in this ersatz mishmash can stand up next to the truths of real science, either for human drama and suspense or for intellectual stimulation and meditation-making. Science is the living dynamic creature which is feeding the fiction writer; and it is science which yearns for and deserves the high regard of men.[4]

The last thing which would have occurred to Dr Beck, one

suspects, was that there might be science-fiction writers who could teach him lessons in the art of metaphor. Yet he is quite right to argue that novels which claim to be scientific while travestying the standards of real science do no good to anybody. Beck's kind of prejudice is, perhaps, less harmful to the genre than the enthusiasm of those educators who would welcome it into the curriculum despite what they take to be its literary third-rateness. In his best-selling *Future Shock* (1970), for example, Alvin Toffler outlines a programme of 'futurist studies' in which SF is an essential constituent:

> Science fiction is held in low regard as a branch of literature, and perhaps it deserves this critical contempt. But if we view it as a kind of sociology of the future, rather than as literature, science fiction has immense value as a mind-stretching force for the creation of the habit of anticipation.[5]

To write like this is simply to evade the question of literary value. If one really believes that science fiction acts as a 'mind-stretching force', then it is impossible to hold that critical contempt for it is justified. As a 'future-oriented' literature which is readily accessible to the young, science fiction has come to feature very widely in history, philosophy, politics, and sociology courses, usually in conjunction with other material. Yet the instructor who shares Toffler's attitude is simply exploiting SF for his own ends, rather than adequately and responsibly teaching it. Science fiction *is* a mode of literature, and courses which make use of it, whatever the context, cannot opt out of the business of artistic judgements.

SF is indeed an interdisciplinary subject, which at times spans the gaps between the 'two cultures'; but then so are many others. Selected SF novels may be used, as Gregory Benford uses them at the University of California-Irvine, to convey some of the concepts of modern physics to students. More importantly, however, SF may provoke reflection on the social and historical contingencies which have led to an arts/science split where, rationally, none need exist. Science is nothing without imagination, guess-work, value-judgements and the persuasion of one's colleagues. On the other hand, as Matthew Arnold wrote in 'Literature and Science' (1882), 'all learning is scientific which is systematically laid out and followed up to its original sources . . . a genuine humanism is scientific'. Thus the 'two cultures' debate unconvincingly attempts to displace what is essentially a political conflict into the realm of fundamental ideas. It may be added that SF can be as validly and 'scientifically' used to introduce the student to (say) contemporary East European literature and society, as to introduce him or her to 'physics without tears'.

As Hillegas' pessimism in 1967 may be taken to suggest, the 'two cultures' debate stimulated good intentions among teachers, but it did not actually produce many SF courses. Two further factors were needed for this: student demand, and the willingness to comply with it. Campus militancy in Britain and America in the late 1960s had an inherently populist character. (One British student received national publicity in the educational press for demanding to be allowed to study comics rather than Pope.) Science fiction was a 'relevant' and 'non-élitist' literature, tending to confirm rather than to affront the student's sense of belonging to a new generation with a unique identity. For the more far-sighted, too, it was a radical mode of writing, capable of challenging and transcending existing social norms. For the first time, SF writers became culture-heroes for a large section of American youth. In the universities where the experiment was first tried, it quickly became apparent that science-fiction courses could be enormously, even embarrassingly, well-subscribed. When the austerities and falling enrolments of the 1970s put some department chairmen in the position of supermarket managers desperately searching for new lines of goods, most of the earlier resistance to including SF in the curriculum was quickly dropped. If business, agriculture, and physics majors were willing to come to the English department to take these courses (together with film studies, or children's literature, or courses on the thriller) as one of their compulsory humanities options, then who would gainsay them? It may be that the invasion of US universities by science-fiction courses had something fortuitous, and almost freakish, about it. The courses were by and large adopted quickly, without the rethinking necessary to fully overcome the academic conservatism of which Hillegas wrote in 1967. In their present state, they might be as easily jettisoned in a return to the 'basics', or to a 'core curriculum', in the study of English.

Consolidation and canon-formation

The need for the immediate future, then, is for consolidation in SF teaching – and, to a lesser extent, in criticism and scholarship. Consolidation implies a recognition that SF is, first and foremost, a species of imaginative writing, but it does not mean compromise with those elements of traditional literary ideology which are inappropriate to it. Science fiction is not part of 'high literature', nor is it undifferentiated mass entertainment. It does not compete for attention with Shakespeare and Milton, Eliot and Joyce, but it is not indifferent to them, either. To get to know it as a literary mode is to begin to read the great writers of the past differently. On the one hand, they appear as creators of imaginary kingdoms, cities, gardens, and islands which bear a certain relation to reality; on the other, they are ornaments of the 'literary tradition' who – we may be forcibly reminded – have reached their present eminence by widely differing routes. No doubt there were people at the time of the First Folio, or of Dryden's translation of *Antony and Cleopatra* into rhyming couplets, who complained that Shakespeare was being made 'respectable'. The Elizabethan drama, like science fiction, began life as a paraliterary form; Joyce's novels did not. The study of contemporary writing from outside the 'élite' tradition brings us closer, perhaps, than does the study of acknowledged modern masters to the process by which a literary heritage is constituted, and to the way in which it changes.

Though it is imaginative writing, SF cannot be mistaken for an 'art for art's sake', since its contacts with the intellectual realities of science, politics, and society are too close. (It certainly provides a home for aesthetically-minded as well as 'utilitarian' writers – for Ballard and Delany as well as Asimov and Clarke – but that is another matter.) SF is responsive to modern society and tends to look to satisfying visions of the future, rather than of a sentimentalized past, for its intimations of an ideal state. This, of course, is its appeal for teachers in non-literary subjects, who nearly always place it in what, borrowing from Toffler, might be called a 'futurist studies' context. Just as historians and sociologists write about such forms as the nineteenth-century novel with, at times, more authority than the literary critics, so should one expect major contributions to science-fiction studies from many places other than English departments. But to pretend that its speculative and propagandist content somehow lessens the impact that it ought to have in the literary field is to fall back on a concept of 'pure' literature which is an evasion of the divided realities of creative expression in our century. Teaching SF, it may be added, is different from teaching the more self-contained literary modes (such as modern poetry) in that it is impossible, as well as undesirable, to maintain the illusion that there is *one* kind of knowledge involved, which the teacher has access to and the students, initially, do not. A class on, say, *The Left Hand of Darkness* – ranging from fictional structures to feminism, diplomacy, foretelling, personal relationships, polar exploration, Taoism, and the likely scientific principles of the Chabe stove – will be rich in opportunities for students to pool their knowledge and educate one another, and perhaps their teacher as well.

SF courses in English departments are normally run on either thematic or historical lines. The main organizational question involved is likely to be that of the choice of texts. (Here I shall concentrate on the choice of works of fiction;

many teachers, however, would supplement these with some non-fictional works of popular science, and there are often opportunities for films to be shown and discussed.) Canon-formation is implicit in any decision to select certain texts for literary study; in science fiction, as a contemporary literature with a brief history in which no authors (except perhaps Wells and Verne) hold an unchallenged place, an individual teacher's decision may be very much more significant than it would be in a course on the Romantic poets. Often this significance will not be confined to the SF genre itself. A decision to teach *Frankenstein*, for example, involves a commentary on all other courses in which *Frankenstein* is taught (e.g. 'The Female Novel', 'The Gothic Novel'), or might be but is usually not taught ('The Nineteenth-Century Novel').

Mark R. Hillegas lists the books that he taught in his 1962 course at Colgate as follows:

> H.G. Wells: five of the 'scientific romances'
> Edward Bellamy: *Looking Backward*
> Olaf Stapledon: *Star Maker*
> B.F. Skinner: *Walden Two*
> Fyodor Dostoyevsky: 'The Grand Inquisitor'
> E.M. Forster: 'The Machine Stops'
> Yevgeny Zamyatin: *We*
> Aldous Huxley: *Brave New World*
> Karel Čapek: *War with the Newts*
> George Orwell: *Nineteen Eighty-Four*
> C.S. Lewis: the space trilogy
> William Golding: *Lord of the Flies*
> Walter M. Miller, Jr: *A Canticle for Leibowitz*

Though it contains works by two writers (Olaf Stapledon and Walter M. Miller, Jr) then little known outside the SF community, this is by any standards a heavily 'mainstream' course, oriented towards writers of established reputation as realistic novelists and social thinkers. Hillegas concedes that this was in part (though, one suspects, only in part) a tactical gesture, aimed at making a new course acceptable.

Such considerations are very much less likely to bother teachers today.

The most adequate guide to the 'canon' which is constituted by science-fiction teaching today is a survey of seventy-seven courses compiled by Jack Williamson in 1974.[6] Over 300 books were recorded at least once in the survey. On the other hand, four of Hillegas' choices (two by Wells and one each by Huxley and Miller) appeared among the dozen most popular texts. These were as follows:

Isaac Asimov: *I, Robot* (prescribed on 11 courses)
Ray Bradbury: *The Martian Chronicles* (14)
Robert A. Heinlein: *The Moon is a Harsh Mistress* (12)
——: *Stranger in a Strange Land* (21)
Frank Herbert: *Dune* (16)
Aldous Huxley: *Brave New World* (15)
Ursula K. Le Guin: *The Left Hand of Darkness* (15)
Walter M. Miller, Jr: *A Canticle for Leibowitz* (23)
Frederik Pohl and C.M. Kornbluth: *The Space Merchants* (17)
Robert Silverberg, ed.: *Science Fiction Hall of Fame*, Vol. 1 (14)
H.G. Wells: *The Time Machine* (12)
——: *The War of the Worlds* (18)

The diversity suggested by this survey is probably less than it seems. The choice of a particular author (which Williamson did not choose to tabulate) is often more significant than that of an individual work, especially since (as every SF teacher knows) the availability of mass-market paperback titles at a given time is almost impossible to predict. Nevertheless, it is significant that no novel appeared more than twenty-three times in the syllabuses that Williamson studied, and that the second most popular title, *Stranger in a Strange Land*, owes its position more to its short-lived cult reputation than to any general agreement as to its pre-eminence among its author's productions – let alone in SF as a whole.

The main feature of Williamson's list is its very heavy

concentration on post-1940 American SF, at the expense of eliminating non-English language works altogether. This is 'genre' science fiction as we have come to know it – the novels, that is, which sell steadily on paperback shelves in bookstores and which are candidates for Hugo and Nebula awards. In some cases their choice may indicate no more than the teacher's sense of what is most accessible to first-year American students. Behind such tactical considerations, however, there lies a major intellectual issue. For those teachers who approach SF primarily as a cultural phenomenon of our times, the emphasis on American writers is not misplaced. Nowhere in the world (not even in the USSR) is there a contemporary SF literature whose development has been wholly free of American influence. From the point of view of the comparatist and the literary historian, however, the choice of second-rate American works in place of European classics of the kind preferred by Hillegas is an index of cultural chauvinism. There is no need, in the present context, to engage in an attempt to arbitrate between these two points of view, since to do so would involve the whole conception of 'science fiction' which is the subject of the preceding chapters. The genre may be taught either as a branch of American writing and culture, or as a genuinely comparative topic in 'world literature'. What is important in educational terms is that the teacher should clearly set out his own assumptions and, where possible, initiate full discussion of the issues involved. Personal experience suggests that the study of a contemporary European writer such as Stanislaw Lem (translations of whose works were not yet widely available in paperback at the time of Williamson's survey) can quickly dispel the illusion that the best science fiction is necessarily that produced in the US. And the choice of a few early texts, from Lucian to the nineteenth century, not only proves stimulating in itself but greatly helps students to confront and question their own implicit notions as to what science fiction is.

The strange and the familiar

Students who enrol in an SF course do not necessarily know much about the genre. Many, in fact, feel quite ignorant about it, despite its apparent accessibility to them. As with other forms of popular literature, it is a mistake to confuse the 'consumer' or 'fan' with the potential student, although the two categories quite often overlap. In part, the teacher of SF, as of any other literature, is concerned to familiarize the students with the material – to make it part of their mental landscapes. He must necessarily be an advocate of the genre to which he is suggesting that they give their time. Such advocacy, however, is unlikely to stress those aspects of SF which make it appear to be 'easy reading'. The teacher will be aware of his own and his students' susceptibility to literary stereotypes, which may turn an alien world into an unthinking copy of our own world. He will also be aware of the various ways in which a 'literature of ideas' may flatter intellectuals and, especially in recent writing, the intellectual young. Teaching SF involves an effort to make the more accessible works appear strange (above all, by bringing to light techniques and conventions which are usually taken for granted), as well as to make the less accessible works familiar.

This dialectic of strangeness and familiarity may serve, in fact, as a metaphor for the nature of any pedagogic discipline. Nineteenth-century humanist education introduced its students to the literature of a culturally, historically, and linguistically alien world – that of classical Greece – which, nevertheless, was held to constitute their essential and ideal heritage. The scientific education pioneered by T.H. Huxley presented, in a rigorously abstract and 'defamiliarized' form, knowledge of the empirical, material world. Similarly, the study of contemporary literature and culture must achieve a certain distance from the objects of its scrutiny if it is to justify itself; not infrequently, this has led to a baffling and self-defeating theoreticism. Where contemporary 'high' literature is concerned, the defamiliarizing apparatus of literary criticism is applied to works which, in their relationship to ordinary social discourse, are themselves often highly enigmatic and oblique. Science fiction is not enigmatic in this way. Instead, as a popular mode of writing, it proclaims itself as being *about* the strange rather than itself constituting the strange. It may, perhaps, be regarded as a 'thinking machine' (or an imagination-machine) for our age. Through the fictive device of the 'working model' it examines our responses to alien worlds and situations which, though they are make-believe, anticipate the kinds of alienness to which we may have to respond in our own lives. Thus the decision to study science fiction directs our attention neither to a fixed past (the classical tradition), nor to a fixed present embodied in 'laws' of nature, but to an open-ended and changing future.

The imagination of unfamiliar realities is a matter of narrative technique, since the alienness of the experience must be evoked within the familiar structures of storytelling. At the same time, it gives substance to that awareness of transformation, both actual and potential, which is implicit in twentieth-century life. Thus, although literary experiments and innovations will, one hopes, be involved, the area occupied by a science-fiction course is wider and less well-charted than that which has come to be conventionally associated with 'literature'. Innovations and alternative possibilities in such fields as politics, sociology, technology, biology, and psychology will all form part of the discussion. There is a sense in which every overall conception of a future or parallel world, like every conception of the past, simply documents the present in which we live. A science-fiction course will show the various levels of obviousness and subtlety at which writers do this. Undoubtedly it will conclude that some of the 'new worlds' are bogus ones (though any novel which appears to the instructor to be irredeemably bogus is, in my opinion, unsuitable for teaching). Yet the desirability and the possibility of such transformations of reality – the obstacles and the inertia that they would have to sweep away – are rehearsed when we read science fiction. To explore such dramatized conjunctions of the strange and the familiar, and to evaluate them – politically, aesthetically, morally, and even scientifically – might be the aim of an SF course.

NOTES

Where indicated, full bibliographical details of the works cited will be found in the appropriate section of the Bibliography.

The following abbreviations have been adopted:

SFS	=	*Science-Fiction Studies.*
JHJ	=	Samuel R. Delany, *The Jewel-Hinged Jaw*, Berkley Windhover, New York 1978.
MSF	=	Darko Suvin, *Metamorphoses of Science Fiction*, Yale University Press, New Haven and London, 1979.
SF	=	*Science Fiction: A Collection of Critical Essays*, ed. Mark Rose, Prentice-Hall, Englewood Cliffs, N.J. 1976.
SF:ACG	=	*Science Fiction: A Critical Guide*, ed. Patrick Parrinder, Longman, London and New York, 1979.

Introduction

1 [Sir Walter Scott], 'Remarks on Frankenstein. . .', *Blackwood's Edinburgh Magazine*, ii. no. 12 (March 1818), p. 620.
2 See chapter 7, note 1.

3   See Todorov (Bibliography 3), and Christine Brooke-
    Rose, 'Historical genres/theoretical genres: a discus-
    sion of Todorov on the fantastic', *New Literary History*,
    viii, no. 1 (Autumn 1976), pp. 145–58.

1   Working daydreams, workshop definitions

1   Quoted by Sam Moskowitz, 'That early coinage of "sci-
    ence fiction" ', *SFS*, iii, pt 3 (November 1976), p. 313.
2   *Blackwood's Edinburgh Magazine*, ii, no. 12 (March 1818),
    p. 614.
3   *The Science Fiction of Edgar Allan Poe*, ed. Harold
    Beaver, Penguin Books, Harmondsworth, 1976, p. 64.
4   Ketterer, *The Rationale of Deception in Poe*, Louisiana
    State University Press, Baton Rouge and London,
    1979, pp. 86–90.
5   'Jules Verne revisited', *T.P.'s Weekly*, 9 October 1903,
    p. 589.
6   *The Letters of Robert Louis Stevenson*, ed. Sidney Colvin,
    Methuen, London, 1901, ii. p. 299.
7   Stevenson, 'A gossip on romance', in *Memories and Por-
    traits* (1887).
8   Darko Suvin, 'On what is and is not an SF narration',
    SFS, v, pt 1 (March 1978), p. 50.
9   Gernsback's unpublished letters to Wells with Wells's
    marginalia are in the Wells Collection at the University
    of Illinois Library.
10 Quoted in Carter (Bibliography 2), p. 11.
11 *JHJ*, p. 260.
12 Heinlein, in Davenport (Bibliography 2), p. 22.
13 Heinlein, 'On the writing of speculative fiction', in *Of
    Worlds Beyond*, ed. Lloyd Arthur Eshbach, Dobson,
    London, 1965, p. 17.
14 John W. Campbell, Jr, 'The science of science fiction
    writing', in Eshbach, *op. cit.*, pp. 103–4.

15 Atheling, *More Issues at Hand* (Bibliography 2), p. 14.
16 *Ibid.*, pp. 99–100.
17 *JHJ*, p. 208.
18 Suvin, 'On what is and is not an SF narration', p. 45.
19 C.S. Lewis, 'On Science Fiction', in *SF*, pp. 111–12.
20 Samuel R. Delany, *The Einstein Intersection*, Garland Publishing, New York and London, 1975, p. 39.
21 *Ibid.*, p. 133.

2 The sociology of the genre

1 For a listing of sociological studies of the type described here, see Clareson (Bibliography 1), Section 1.
2 But see Darko Suvin, 'Russian SF and its utopian tradition', in *MSF*, pp. 243-69; Christopher Priest, 'British science fiction', in *SF:ACG*, pp. 187–202; and Franz Rottensteiner, 'European Science Fiction', in *SF:ACG*, pp. 203–26.
3 Scholes (Bibliography 2), p. 35.
4 Toffler (Bibliography 4), p. 384.
5 Sanders, 'The disappearance of character', in *SF:ACG*, pp. 131–47.
6 Angenot, 'Jules Verne: the last happy utopianist,' in *SF:ACG*, pp. 18–33.
7 Lucien Goldmann, *The Hidden God*, trans. Philip Thody, Routledge & Kegan Paul, London, 1976.
8 Patrick Parrinder, 'Science fiction and the scientific world-view', in *SF:ACG*, pp. 67–89.
9 Klein, 'Discontent in American science fiction', *SFS*, iv, pt 1 (March 1977), 3–13.
10 *Ibid.*, p. 8.
11 Berger (Bibliography 4), p. 239.
12 *Ibid.*, p. 242.
13 See Linda Fleming, 'The American SF sub-culture', *SFS*, iv, pt 3 (November 1977), pp. 263–71.
14 I am grateful to Brian Stableford for stimulating my

thinking on this subject. See his adaptation of Robert
Escarpit's distinction between 'connoisseur reading'
and 'consumer reading' in Stableford (Bibliography 4),
p. 30.

15 Jeffrey R. Hohman, 'Stocking and selling SF', *Publishers' Weekly*, ccix, no. 24 (14 June 1976), p. 60.
16 Fleming, *op. cit.*, p. 267.
17 Shippey, 'The cold war in science fiction, 1940–1960', in *SF:ACG*, pp. 90–109.
18 *Ibid.*, pp. 107, 108. Compare Fleming, *op. cit.*, p. 269.
19 Cawelti (Bibliography 3), pp. 35–6.
20 The phrase is from Cawelti, *op. cit.*, p. 299.
21 Angenot (Bibliography 3), pp. 4–5 (my translation).
22 See, e.g., Darko Suvin, 'Introduction' to 'The sociology of science fiction,' (Bibliography 4), p. 227.
23 Angenot (Bibliography 3), p. 49.

3 Science Fiction as romance

1 Richard Chase, *The American Novel and Its Tradition*, Doubleday, Garden City, N.Y., 1957, p. 13.
2 Northrop Frye, 'The archetypes of literature', *Kenyon Review*, xiii no. 1 (1951), pp. 92 ff.
3 Frye (Bibliography 3), p. 49.
4 *Ibid.*, p. 33.
5 Beer (Bibliography 3), p. 8.
6 T.E. Hulme, *Speculations*, ed. Herbert Read, Routledge & Kegan Paul, London, 1936, p. 140.
7 This idea is implicit in the titles of various critical books on SF. See Barron (Bibliography 1), Knight, and Nicholls (Bibliography 2).
8 Zamyatin, *Herbert Wells*, reprinted in *H.G. Wells: The Critical Heritage*, ed. Patrick Parrinder, Routledge and Kegan Paul, London & Boston, 1972, p. 260.
9 See, e.g., *Science Fiction: Contemporary Mythology: The*

SFWA–SFRA Anthology, ed. Patricia Warrick, Martin Harry Greenberg, Joseph Olander, Harper & Row, New York, 1978.

10 Sontag, 'The imagination of disaster', in *SF*, p. 127.

11 Propp (Bibliography 3), p. 19.

12 *Ibid.*, pp. 20–1.

13 *Ibid.*, p. 105.

14 Cawelti (Bibliography 3), p. 1.

15 Cesare Segre, 'Narrative structures and literary history', *Critical Inquiry*, iii, no. 2 (Winter 1976), pp. 274–5.

16 See Sanders, 'The disappearance of character', in *SF:ACG*, pp. 131–47; and C.S. Lewis, 'On science fiction', in *SF*, p. 108.

17 Ursula K. Le Guin, 'Myth and archetype in science fiction', *Parabola*, i. no. 4 (Fall 1976), p. 45.

18 Wells, Preface to *The Scientific Romances of H.G. Wells*, Gollancz, London, 1933, p. viii.

19 John Huntington, 'Science fiction and the future', in *SF*, p. 166.

20 C.S. Lewis, 'An expostulation', in *Holding Your Eight Hands: An Anthology of Science Fiction Verse*, ed. Edward Lucie-Smith, Rapp & Whiting, London, 1970, p. 58.

21 Beer (Bibliography 3), p. 47.

22 Ursula K. Le Guin, *The Left Hand of Darkness*, Panther, London, 1973, p. 9.

23 *Ibid.*, pp. 201–2.

24 *Ibid.*, pp. 200–1.

25 I am indebted for some of the details of the foregoing discussion to my student Mr Anthony Paré.

26 For further discussion on this point see Patrick Parrinder, 'Delany inspects the word-beast', *SFS*, vi, pt 3 (November 1979), pp. 337–41.

4 Science Fiction as fable

1 Joanna Russ, 'Towards an aesthetic of science fiction', *SFS*, ii, pt 2 (July 1975), pp. 112–19.

2 Angus Fletcher, *Allegory: The Theory of a Symbolic Mode*,

Cornell University Press, Ithaca and London, 1964, p. 2.

3 Darko Suvin, 'Preliminary theses on allegory', *Umjetnost Mjecu* (Zagreb), xxi, nos. 1/3 (1977), pp. 197–9.

4 For example, Williams (Bibliography 3), and John Colmer, *Coleridge to Catch-22: Images of Society*, Macmillan, London, 1978.

5 Amis (Bibliography 2), p. 54.

6 For example, Brian Ash, *Faces of the Future*, Elek, London, 1975; Harold L. Berger, *Science Fiction and the New Dark Age*, Bowling Green University Popular Press, Bowling Green, Ohio, 1976; and Toffler (Bibliography 4).

7 Robert Bloch, 'Imagination and modern social criticism', in Davenport (Bibliography 2).

8 Richard Lupoff, 'Science fiction hawks and doves', *Ramparts*, x, no. 8 (February 1972), pp. 25–30.

9 Wells, Preface to *The Scientific Romances*, p. viii.

10 Suvin, 'Estrangement and cognition', in *MSF*, pp. 3–15. For discussions of cognitive estrangement, see Scholes (Bibliography 2), pp. 46–7, and Delany, *JHJ*, pp. 255–61.

11 See V. Shklovsky, 'The Resurrection of the Word', in *20th-Century Studies*, nos. 7/8 (December 1972), pp. 41–7, and various texts reprinted in *Théorie de la littérature*, ed. Tzvetan Todorov, Seuil, Paris, 1965. For a commentary see Fredric Jameson, *The Prison-House of Language*, Princeton University Press, Princeton NJ, 1974, pp. 56–8.

12 Quoted by Suvin in *MSF*, p. 54.

13 Quoted in *ibid.*, p. 6.

14 Jameson, *op. cit.*, p. 58.

15 *Arnold Bennett and H.G. Wells*, ed. Harris Wilson, University of Illinois Press, Unbana Ill., 1960, p. 265.

16 Quoted in *JHJ*, p. 278. I have found Delany's discussion highly suggestive at this point.

17 Stanley G. Weinbaum, 'A Martian Odyssey', in *Science Fiction Hall of Fame*, ed. Robert Silverberg, Avon, New

York, 1970. p. 18.

18 Bloch's collected works are published in German by
    Suhrkamp Verlag. For a useful introduction to his
    thought see L. Hurbon, *Ernst Bloch: Utopie et Espérance*,
    Editions du Cerf, Paris, 1974.

19 Rabkin (Bibliography 3), p. 147.

20 *MSF*, pp. 61–2.

21 For the first alternative, see Walsh (Bibliography 2),
    and Harold L. Berger, *op. cit.* For the second, see *SFS*,
    ii, pt 3 (November 1975), ('The science fiction of Ursula
    K. Le Guin'), *passim*.

22 Lewis, *The Abolition of Man*, Oxford University Press,
    London, 1943, pp. 35, 30.

23 J.B.S. Haldane, *Daedalus: or Science and the Future*,
    Kegan Paul, Trench, Trubner, London, 1924. p. 93.

24 See Gary Werskey, *The Visible College*, Allen Lane, Lon-
    don, 1978.

25 H.G. Wells, *Things to Come*, Macmillan, New York,
    1935, pp. 154–5.

26 J.D. Bernal, *The World, the Flesh, and the Devil*, Cape
    Editions, London, 1970, p. 71.

27 *MSF*, p. 217.

28 H.G. Wells, *The War of the Worlds*, Penguin Books,
    Harmondsworth, 1946, p. 191.

29 Werskey, *op. cit.*, p. 335.

30 Steven Weinberg, *The First Three Minutes*, André
    Deutsch, London, 1977, p. 154.

31 Ursula K. Le Guin, *The Left Hand of Darkness*, Panther,
    London, 1973, p. 83.

32 *Ibid.*, p. 175.

33 *Ibid.*, pp. 96–7.

5 Science Fiction as epic

1 *MSF*, p. 78.

2 Pound, *ABC of Reading*, quoted by Paul Merchant, *The
   Epic*, Methuen, London, 1971, p. 1.

3 See Canary (Bibliography 4).

4   H.G. Wells, 'Fiction about the future', typescript in the Wells Collection, University of Illinois Library, of a talk broadcast over Australian radio on 29 December 1938.

5   Georg Lukács, *The Theory of the Novel*, trans. Anna Bostock, Merlin Press, London, 1971, pp. 46, 78ff.

6   Georg Lukács, *The Historical Novel*, trans. Hannah and Stanley Mitchell, Merlin Press, London, 1969. p. 63.

7   *Ibid.*, p. 189.

8   Mark R. Hillegas, 'Second thoughts on the course in science fiction', in McNelly (Bibliography 2), p. 17.

9   H.G. Wells, *The Time Machine*, Heinemann, London, 1949, p. 90.

10 George Locke, 'Wells in three volumes?', *SFS*, iii, pt 3, pp. 282–6.

11 *The Time Machine*, pp. 30–2.

12 See Charles Elkins, 'Science fiction versus futurology', *SFS*, vi, pt 1 (March 1979), pp. 20–31.

13 Isaac Asimov, quoted in John Huntington, 'Science fiction and the future', in *SFS*, p. 165.

14 J.B.S. Haldane, *Possible Worlds and Other Essays*, Chatto & Windus, London, 1927, p. 292.

15 *Ibid.*, p. 295.

16 Canary (Bibliography 4), p. 85.

17 See R.D. Mullen, 'Blish, Van Vogt, and the uses of Spengler', *Riverside Quarterly*, iii (August 1968), pp. 172ff.

18 Bernal, *The World, the Flesh, and the Devil*, Cape Editions, London, 1970, p. 46.

19 Robert A. Heinlein, *Orphans of the Sky*, Berkley Medallion, New York, 1970, pp. 127–8.

20 *The Best Short Stories of J.G. Ballard*, Holt, Rinehart & Winston, New York, 1978, p. 159.

6   Imitation and novelty: an approach through SF language

1   *Blackwood's Edinburgh Magazine*, ii, no. 2 (March 1818) p. 619.

2 Basil Williams in the *Athenaeum*, reprinted in *H.G. Wells: The Critical Heritage*, ed. Patrick Parrinder, Routledge & Kegan Paul, London and Boston, 1972, p. 57.

3 Arthur C. Clarke, *Rendezvous with Rama*, Pan Books, London and Sydney, 1974, p. 190.

4 Yevgeny Zamyatin, *We*, trans. Mirra Ginsburg, Bantam Books, New York, 1972, pp. 8–9.

5 *JHJ*, p. 36.

6 Delany, *The American Shore* (Bibliography 2), p. 58.

7 Samuel R. Delany, 'Science fiction and "literature" or the conscience of the king', *Analog Science Fiction/Science Fact* (May 1979), p. 78.

8 Angenot (Bibliography 4), pp. 9-19.

9 *Ibid.*, p. 15.

10 Michel Butor, 'The crisis in the growth of science fiction', in *Inventory*, trans. Richard Howard, Cape, London, 1970, p. 231.

11 Tom Shippey, 'The cold war in science fiction, 1940–1960', in *SF:ACG*, p. 91.

12 Kurt Vonnegut, Jr, *The Sirens of Titan*, Coronet Books, London, 1972, p. 7.

13 *Ibid.*, p. 191.

14 *Ibid.*, p. 202.

15 Philip K. Dick, *Martian Time-Slip*, Ballantine Books, New York, 1976, p. 94.

16 *Ibid.*, pp. 126, 133, 141.

17 *Ibid.*, pp. 76–7.

18 Stanislaw Lem, *Solaris*, trans. Joanna Kilmartin and Steve Cox, Arrow Books, London, 1973, p. 1.

19 *Ibid.*, p. 169.

20 *Ibid.*, p. 23.

21 *Ibid.*, p. 170.

22 *Ibid.*, p. 104.

23 *Ibid.*, pp. 160–1.

24 *Ibid.*, p. 192.

25 Darko Suvin, 'Afterword', in *Solaris*, Walker, New York, 1970.

26 *Solaris*, p. 162.

27   *Ibid.*, p. 203.
28   *Ibid.*, p. 204.
29   *Ibid.*, p. 134.

7   The Science-Fiction course

1   Sam Moskowitz, 'The first to teach science fiction in college?', *Publishers' Weekly*, ccx, no. 8 (23 August 1976), p. 8.
2   Mark. R. Hillegas, 'The course in science fiction: a hope deferred', *Extrapolation*, ix, no. 1 (December 1967), pp. 18–21.
3   James Gunn, 'Teaching science fiction', *Publishers' Weekly*, ccix, no. 24 (14 June 1976), p. 62.
4   William S. Beck, *Modern Science and the Nature of Life*, Penguin Books, Harmondsworth, 1961, p. 21.
5   Toffler (Bibliography 4), p. 384.
6   Jack Williamson, 'SF in the classroom', in McNelly (Bibliography 2), p. 12.

SELECT BIBLIOGRAPHY

Keeping up with the secondary literature of science-fiction studies is an increasingly arduous task. The main journals in the field and the *SFRA Newsletter* have review sections in each number. Some books are difficult to obtain outside the USA, though visits to the various bookshops specializing in science fiction and fantasy are usually rewarding, especially where small-press publications and 'fanzines' are concerned.

For the reader who is relatively unfamiliar with SF, further reading should, of course, commence with the texts themselves, and particularly with the authors and works mentioned in the preceding chapters.

No attempt has been made here to list the growing body of critical and bibliographical material on individual authors. Nor have journal articles and chapters in books been listed, except in Bibliography 4. The principal critical and scholarly articles that have been consulted in writing this book are indicated in the Notes.

The Bibliography that follows is in four sections, and represents a personal choice of the most important books embodying our present-day knowledge of science fiction, its criticism and teaching. The bias is an academic and scholarly one, the principal omission being that of the multitude of more-or-less informal contributions by science-fiction writers (following the tradition sketched in chapter 1) to the debate about what SF is and might be.

1 Reference materials

BARRON, NEIL, ed. *Anatomy of Wonder: Science Fiction*, Bowker, New York 1976. An excellent bibliographical and historical guide, listing over 1,100 works of SF from the Renaissance to the present.

CLARESON, THOMAS D.*Science Fiction Criticism: An Annotated Checklist*, Kent State University Press, Kent, Ohio, 1972. A comprehensive list of SF criticism up to 1972.

CLARKE, I.F. *The Tale of the Future*, 3rd edn, Library Association, London, 1978. Annotated bibliography of some 3,900 anticipation tales.

CONTENTO, WILLIAM.*Index to Science Fiction Anthologies and Collections*, G.K. Hall & Co., Boston, 1978.

Extrapolation: A Journal of Science Fiction and Fantasy. Founded by Thomas D. Clareson in 1959, and serving the Modern Language Association seminar on SF and the Science Fiction Research Association, this is the longest-running academic journal of SF.

Foundation. Published by the Science Fiction Foundation, North-East London Polytechnic, this lively British journal is noted for its contributions from SF writers, and for its book reviews.

NICHOLLS, PETER, ed. *The Encyclopaedia of Science Fiction*, Granada, London, 1979. The most up-to-date encyclopaedia of SF.

SCIENCE FICTION RESEARCH ASSOCIATION. The Association holds an annual conference and publishes *SFRA Newsletter* ten times a year. Membership includes subscriptions to *Extrapolation* and *Science-Fiction Studies*. Enquiries to the Treasurer, Elizabeth Cummins Cogell, Humanities Dept., University of Missouri-Rolla, Rolla, Missouri 65401, USA.

Scence-Fiction Studies. Founded in 1973 by R.D. Mullen and Darko Suvin. The leading journal of SF criticism, history, and theory. See also Mullen and Suvin (Bibliography 2).

SUVIN, DARKO. *Russian Science Fiction 1956–74: A Biblio-graphy*, Dragon Press, Elizabethtown, NY, 1976.

TUCK, DONALD H. *The Encyclopaedia of Science Fiction and Fantasy Through 1968*, Vol. 1 (A–L), Advent, Chicago, 1974: Vol. 2 (M–Z), Advent, Chicago, 1978. A comprehensive *Who's Who* to SF, containing around 2,500 entries.

VERSINS, PIERRE. *Encyclopédie de l'Utopie, de la science-fiction et des voyages extraordinaires*, L'Age d'Homme, Lausanne 1972.

2 Literary criticism, history, and theory of Science Fiction

ALDISS, BRIAN W. *Billion Year Spree*, Weidenfeld & Nicolson, London, 1973. A lively, readable and comprehensive history of SF by a leading British novelist.

AMIS, KINGSLEY. *New Maps of Hell*, Gollancz, London, 1961. A pioneering and inimitable, if by now heavily dated, commentary on the field by one of SF's earliest advocates in the literary 'mainstream'.

AQUINO, JOHN. *Science Fiction as Literature*, National Education Association, Washington, DC, 1976. Discusses methods of teaching SF at high-school level.

'ATHELING, WILLIAM, JR' [JAMES BLISH]. *The Issue at Hand*, Advent, Chicago, 1964. *More Issues at Hand*, Advent, Chicago, 1970. Collected reviews by a pioneer of SF criticism in the magazines.

BAILEY, J.O. *Pilgrims Through Space and Time*, Greenwood Press, Westport, Conn., 1972. Pioneering survey of early SF, first published in 1947.

BRETNOR, REGINALD, ed. *Science Fiction, Today and Tomorrow*, Penguin Books, Baltimore, Md, 1975. Essays mainly by SF novelists.

CARTER, PAUL A, *The Creation of Tomorrow*, Columbia University Press, New York, 1977. An excellent, thematically-organized scholarly survey of 'fifty years of magazine science fiction'.

CLARESON, THOMAS D., ed. *SF: The Other Side of Realism*,

Bowling Green University Popular Press, Bowling Green, Ohio, 1971. A compendious collection of critical essays by a very varied group of contributors.

CLARESON, THOMAS D., ed. *Voices for the Future: Essays on Major Science Fiction Writers*, Bowling Green University Popular Press, Bowling Green, Ohio, 1976.

CLARKE, I.F. *Voices Prophesying War, 1763–1984,* Oxford University Press, New York, 1966. Studies the sub-genre of 'future war' stories.

DAVENPORT, BASIL, ed. *The Science Fiction Novel: Imagination and Social Criticism*, 3rd edn, Advent, Chicago, 1969. Important collection of essays by SF writers, first published in 1959.

DELANY, SAMUEL R. *The American Shore*, Dragon Press, Elizabethtown, NY, 1978. A far-sighted theoretical treatise on SF poetics, cast in the form of a sentence-by-sentence analysis of 'Angouleme', a story by Thomas M. Disch.

DELANY, SAMUEL R. *The Jewel-Hinged Jaw: Notes on the Language of Science fiction*, Dragon Press, Elizabethtown, NY, 1977; Berkley Windhover, New York, 1978. A retrospective collection of essays by SF's leading contemporary critic-novelist.

Europe, 55e. année (August-September 1977). Edited by Jacques Goimard. A special number devoted to SF from the French point of view, with many useful articles.

FRANKLIN, H. BRUCE, ed. *Future Perfect: American Science Fiction of the Nineteenth Century*, revised edn, Oxford University Press, New York, 1978. A useful anthology with generous critical commentaries.

GERBER, RICHARD. *Utopian Fantasy*, McGraw-Hill, New York, 1973. Interesting study of twentieth-century utopias, with bibliographical appendices updated from the original (1955) edition.

GUNN, JAMES. *Alternate Worlds: The Illustrated History of Science Fiction*, Prentice-Hall, Englewood Cliffs, NJ, 1975. Useful if slightly parochial history of (twentieth-century American) SF and its antecedents.

GUNN, JAMES, ed. *The Road to Science Fiction: from Gilgamesh to Wells*, Mentor Books, New York, 1977. A highly accessible anthology of extracts from early SF, with introductions and bibliography.

HILLEGAS, MARK R. *The Future as Nightmare: H.G. Wells and the Anti-Utopians*, Oxford University Press, New York, 1967. Studies Wells's influence on Forster, Zamyatin, Orwell, and more recent anti-utopian SF.

KETTERER, DAVID. *New Worlds for Old*, Indiana University Press, Bloomington, Ind., 1974. Studies a number of nineteenth- and twentieth-century SF works as expressions of the 'apocalyptic imagination' in literature.

KNIGHT, DAMON. *In Search of Wonder*, revised edn, Advent, Chicago, 1967. Trenchant criticism and reviewing from within the SF field.

LEWIS, C.S. *Of Other Worlds: Essays and Stories*, ed. Walter Hooper, Geoffrey Bles, London, 1966. Includes Lewis's pioneering essay 'On science fiction', together with other SF items.

MCNELLY, WILLIS E., ed. *Science Fiction: The Academic Awakening*, supplement to *CEA Critic* xxxvii, no. 1 (November 1974). Contains notable essays by Mark R. Hillegas and Jack Williamson on the teaching of SF.

MULLEN, R.D., and SUVIN, DARKO. *Science-Fiction Studies: Selected Articles*, Gregg Press, Boston, 1976. *Science-Fiction Studies: Second Series*, Gregg Press, Boston, 1978. Two collections of reprinted articles from SF's leading academic journal.

NICHOLLS, PETER, ed. *Science Fiction at Large*, Gollancz, London, 1976. Reissued as *Explorations of the Marvellous*, Fontana/Collins, London, 1978. A lecture-series given at the Institute of Contemporary Arts, with notable contributions by Ursula K. Le Guin, John Brunner, Thomas M. Disch, and others.

NICOLSON, MARJORIE HOPE. *Voyages to the Moon*, Macmillan, New York, 1948. Scholarly study of moon voyages from antiquity to the early nineteenth century.

PARRINDER, PATRICK, ed. *Science Fiction: A Critical Guide*,

Longman, London and New York, 1979. Thematic and historical essays by a team of contributors including Mark R. Hillegas, Christopher Priest, Franz Rottensteiner, J.A. Sutherland, T.A. Shippey, Raymond Williams, and the editor.

PHILMUS, ROBERT M. *Into the Unknown: The Evolution of Science Fiction from Francis Godwin to H.G. Wells*, University of California Press, Berkeley, 1970. A pioneering scholarly study of early science fiction.

ROSE, MARK, ed. *Science Fiction: A Collection of Critical Essays*, Prentice-Hall, Englewood Cliffs, NJ, 1976. A well-edited and indispensable volume of reprinted essays in the 'Twentieth-Century Views' series.

SCHOLES, ROBERT. *Structural Fabulation*, University of Notre Dame Press, Notre Dame and London, 1975. Controversial advocacy of SF as 'structural fabulation', a 'fictional criticism of the future'.

SCHOLES, ROBERT, and RABKIN, ERIC S. *Science Fiction: History, Science, Vision*, Oxford University Press, New York, 1977. An uneven but, at best, intelligent and useful survey volume, aimed at the student market.

SUVIN, DARKO. *Metamorphoses of Science Fiction*, Yale University Press, New Haven and London, 1979. A magisterial compilation of essays on SF poetics, and on its history from More's *Utopia* (1516) to Čapek's *War with the Newts* (1936), by one of the genre's most influential critics and theorists.

WALSH, CHAD. *From Utopia to Nightmare*, Geoffrey Bles, London, 1962. Pioneering study of twentieth-century anti-utopian literature.

3   Other relevant works of literary criticism and theory

(This brief listing is confined to works immediately relevant to further reading on the subject of science fiction. A number of other works drawn on in the course of the present book are cited in the Notes.)

ANGENOT, MARC. *Le roman populaire: Recherches en paralittérature*, Les Presses de l'Université du Québec, Montreal, 1975. Outlines the concept of paraliterature and exemplifies it in a series of studies on nineteenth-century French popular fiction.

BEER, GILLIAN. *The Romance*, Methuen, London, 1970. Takes in SF as a modern descendant of the romance genre.

CAWELTI, JOHN G. *Adventure, Mystery, and Romance: Formula-Stories as Art and Popular Culture*, University of Chicago Press, Chicago and London, 1976. Provocative if not wholly satisfying discussion of formulaic elements in various types of popular fiction.

FRYE, NORTHROP. *Anatomy of Criticism*, Princeton University Press, Princeton, NJ, 1957. Fits SF within its comprehensive framework of fictional 'modes' deriving from primitive myth.

PROPP, VLADIMIR. *Morphology of the Folk-Tale*, ed. Svatova Pirkova-Jakobson, Indiana University Research Center in Anthropology, Folklore, and Linguistics, Bloomington, Ind., 1958. The classic Russian Formalist approach to the problem of narrative formulas.

RABKIN, ERIC S. *The Fantastic in Literature*, Princeton University Press, Princeton NJ, 1976. An ambitious, not wholly successful attempt to define the generic boundaries delimiting SF, fantasy, and utopia.

TODOROV, TZVETAN. *Introduction à la littérature fantastique*, Seuil, Paris, 1970. Controversial theoretical delimitation of the genre of the 'fantastic'.

WILLIAMS, RAYMOND. *The Country and the City*, Chatto & Windus, London, 1973. SF works are used to exemplify aspects of modern 'metropolitan' experience.

4 SF and other disciplines

ANGENOT, MARC. 'The absent paradigm: an introduction to the semiotics of science fiction', *SFS* vi, pt 1 (March 1979), pp. 9–19.

BAXTER, JOHN. *Science Fiction in the Cinema*, A.S. Barnes, New York, and Zwemmer, London, 1970. The best book on its subject to date.

BERGER, ALBERT I. 'Science-fiction fans in socio-economic perspective', *SFS* iv, pt 3 (November 1977). pp. 232–46.

CANARY, ROBERT H. 'Science fiction as fictive history', *Extrapolation* xvi, no. 1 (December 1974), pp. 81–95.

CLARESON, THOMAS D., ed. *Many Futures, Many Worlds: Theme and Form in Science Fiction*, Kent State University Press, Kent, Ohio, 1977. An uneven collection, including essays on SF and technology, SF and science, SF and mythology, and on the genre from philosophical, theological, and feminist standpoints.

ELIADE, MIRCEA. 'The occult and the modern world', in *Occultism, Witchcraft, and Cultural Fashions*, University of Chicago Press, Chicago and London, 1976, pp. 47–68. Discusses the quasi-religious aspects of SF cultism.

JOHNSON, WILLIAM, ed. *Focus on the Science Fiction Film*, Prentice-Hall, Englewood Cliffs, NJ, 1972. A retrospective anthology of critical essays.

KNOWLSON, JAMES R. 'Communication with other worlds in fiction', *Philosophical Journal* v (1968), pp. 61ff.

KRUEGER, JOHN R. 'Language and techniques of communication as theme in science fiction', *Linguistics* xxxix (May 1968), pp. 68ff.

NICHOLLS, PETER, ed. *Science Fiction at Large* (see Bibliography 2).

PLANK, ROBERT. *The Emotional Significance of Imaginary Beings*, Chas. C. Thomas, Springfield, Ill., 1968. A psychoanalyst's approach to SF.

Science-Fiction Studies iv, pt 3 (November 1977). Special number on 'The Sociology of Science Fiction'.

STABLEFORD, BRIAN. 'Notes toward a sociology of science fiction', *Foundation* xv (January 1979), pp. 28–41.

TOFFLER, ALVIN. *Future Shock*, Pan Books, London, 1971.

INDEX